LOONEY TUNES

THE ULTIMATE ~~VISUAL~~ GUIDE
daffy

LONDON, NEW YORK, MUNICH,
MELBOURNE AND DELHI

Senior Editor Simon Beecroft
Art Editors Guy Harvey and Nick Avery
Designer Christopher Branfield
Editor Julia March
Category Publisher Alex Kirkham
Art Director Mark Richards
Publishing Manager Cynthia O'Neill Collins
Production Nicola Torode
US Editor Margaret Parrish
DTP Designer Eric Shapland

First published in Great Britain in 2003 by
Dorling Kindersley Limited,
80 Strand, London WC2R 0RL
A Penguin Company

03 04 05 10 9 8 7 6 5 4 3 2 1

 Copyright © 2003 Warner Bros. Entertainment Inc.
LOONEY TUNES and all related characters and elements
are trademarks of and © Warner Bros. Entertainment Inc.
WB SHIELD: (tm) & © Warner Bros. Entertainment Inc.
(s03)

Page Design Copyright © Dorling Kindersley Ltd

All rights reserved. No part of this publication may be reproduced,
stored in a retrieval system, or transmitted in any form or by any
means, electronic, mechanical, photocopying, recording, or otherwise,
without the prior written permission of the copyright owner.

A CIP record for this book is available from the British Library.

ISBN 0-7513-2846-4

Color reproduction by Media Development and Printing Ltd
Printed and bound in Italy by L.E.G.O.

Discover more at
www.dk.com

LOONEY TUNES

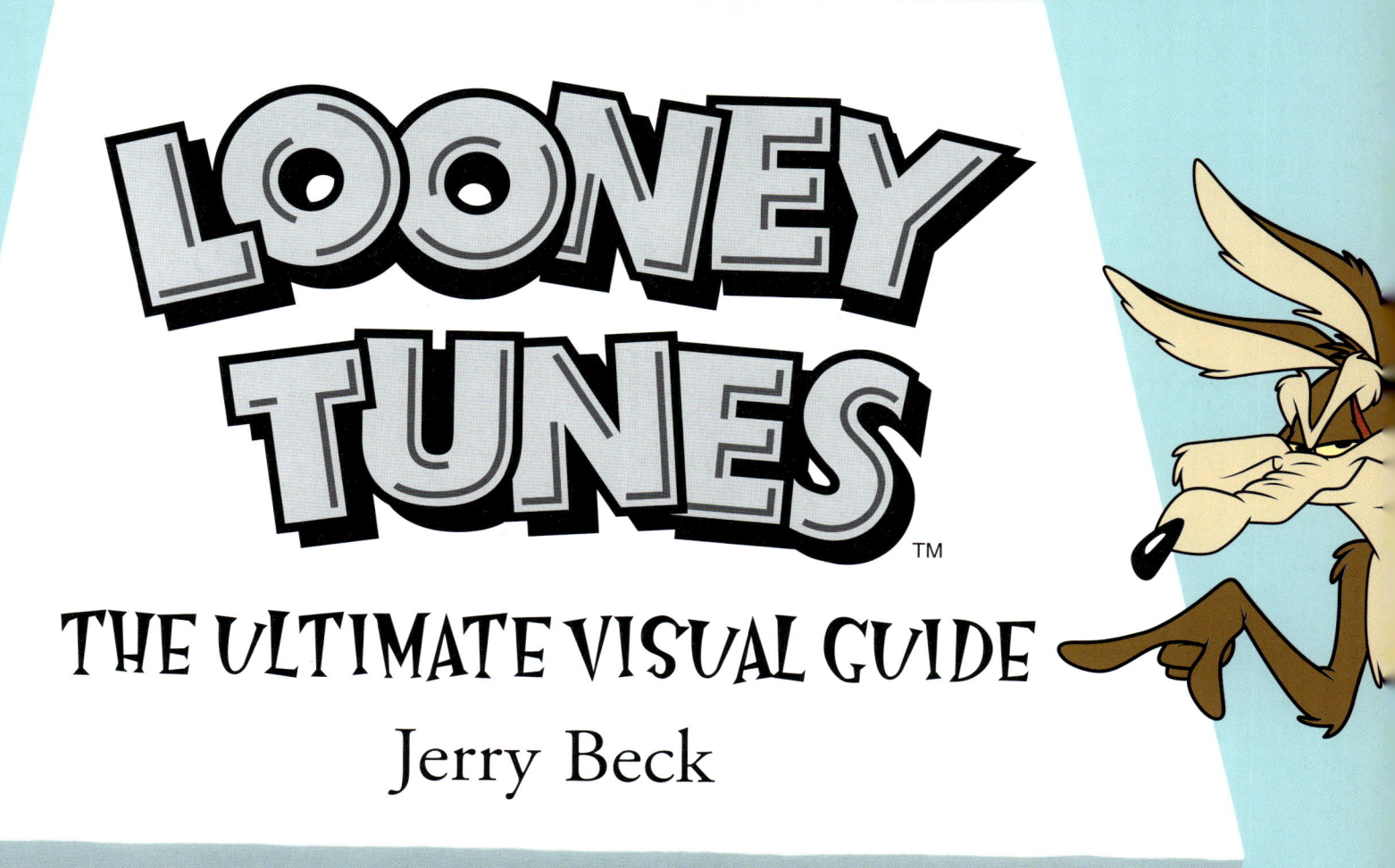

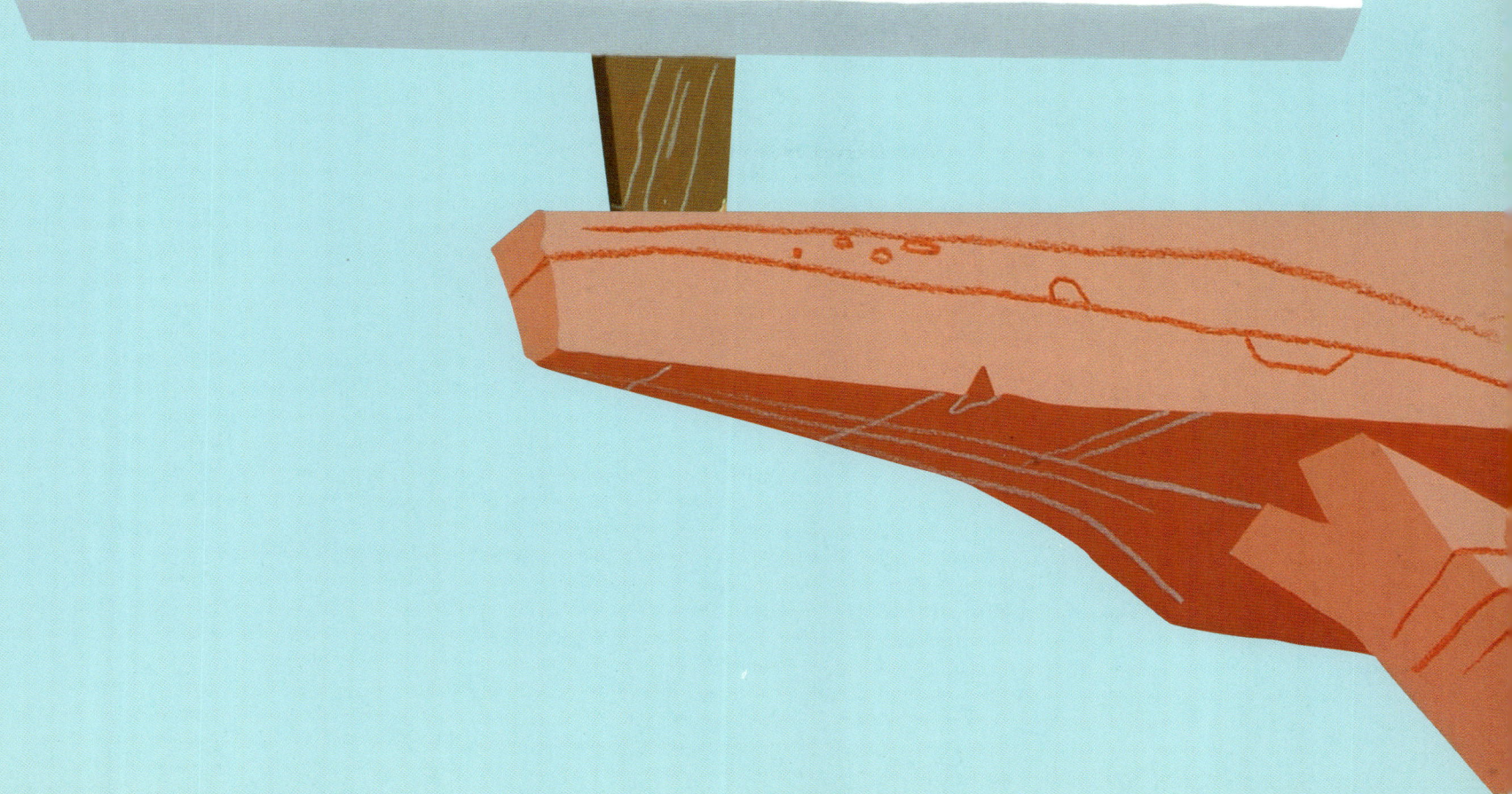

THE ULTIMATE VISUAL GUIDE

Jerry Beck

CONTENTS

Foreword 6
Under the Spotlight 8

BUGS AND DAFFY

Bugs Bunny 12
Screwball Bunny 14
Bugs' Burrow 16
Bugs in Drag 18
Here Comes Trouble 20
Truly Daffy 22
His Bitter Half 24
Daffy's Delusions 26
Daffy Vs. Bugs 28

THE COMPANY

P-P-Porky Pig 32
B-B-Big Deal! 34
Elmer Fudd 36
Tasmanian Devil 38
Yosemite Sam 40
Pepe Le Pew 42
Marvin the Martian 44
Foghorn Leghorn 46
Speedy Gonzales 48
Dazzling Dames 50
Gag Reflex 52

THE BEST OF ENEMIES

Canary 56
Puddy Tat 57
Sylvester and Tweety 58
Thufferin' Thuccotash! 60
Good Relations 62
Road Runner & Wile E. Coyote 64
Desert Hunt 66
Acme Corp. 68
Supergenius 70
Ralph and Sam 72
Cautionary Tales 74

PUMAS AND GOPHERS AND BEARS, OH MY!

Sniffles 78
Cecil Tortoise 79
Goofy Gophers 80
The Three Bears 82
Birds of a Feather 84
Pete Puma 86
Gossamer 87
Cool Cat & Co 88
Slap Happy 90

UNFORGETTABLE

Show Stoppers 94
Menace to Society 96
Feline Friends 98
Canine Corps 100
Cheese Lovers 102
Mini-Toons 104
Before Color 106

ANIMATED WORLD

Cartoon Makers	110
Voices and Music	112
Background Art	114
Supporting Features	116
The Making of a Classic	118
Creating the Look	120
Animated Stars	122
The Good Fight	124

LONG LIVE LOONEY TUNES

Merchandise	128
Publishing	130
Back In Action 1	132
Back In Action 2	134
To the Future	136
Index	138
Acknowledgments	144

FOREWORD

Since many refer to me as Bugs Bunny's agent, I take a particular interest in our Looney Tunes publishing because it reflects our characters in the act of being themselves. It's our heritage and our future—Bugs' future—and he's a long way from retirement. As Chuck Jones might have said, Bugs isn't "hare today and gone tomorrow."

There aren't many wiseacre bunnies, neurotic ducks, bigmouth roosters, pantless pigs, obsessed coyotes, homicidal canaries, and romantic skunks that have made themselves part of the language of our culture. Just calling somebody "Looney Tunes" brings up a vision of happy anarchy, a topsy-turvy world that's a lot like our own but still makes sense. That's Looney Tunes. The terms "doc," "despicable," "putty tat," "suffererin' succotash," and "kill the wabbit!" all conjure images of some of animation's funniest and most human moments, delivered by a cast of hundreds (thousands if you count fleas and ants).

These days everybody wants a piece of them. The Looney Tunes as products were always popular (Leon Schlesinger first licensed them way back when). Then in 1990, when we created Warner Bros. Consumer Products, they became a "mega" commercial success as we extended the characters' wit and charm into things that people could have and hold, a symbol of their identification with the characters. From apparel to interactive games, to books and beyond, I'm proud to be affiliated in this way with the Looney Tunes characters.

This book is a salute to the great Looney Tunes directors, animators, artists, writers, composers, sound effects wizards and all the other talented and dedicated people who helped bring this unique brand of humor to the screen and who added a new dimension to the vocabulary of film comedy.

"From crib to crypt." Sounds grim, but that's how someone once referred to the breadth of the Looney Tunes' audience (comforting, finally, to have a demographic classification in which I feel fully included). Speaking purely as Bugs' agent, I hope this beautifully designed Dorling Kindersley book is well-received; as a Looney Tunes fan, I know that if you bought this volume, you're passionate about these cartoons and their history—past, present, and future. Thanks for sharing our passion.

Dan Romanelli
President, Warner Bros.
Worldwide Consumer Products

UNDER THE SPOTLIGHT

Here they come, from all corners of the animal kingdom (and sometimes farther afield)—the Looney Tunes. And they bite! Like all of us, they are at the mercy of their instincts. There's no love lost between Bugs, Daffy, Yosemite Sam, and the rest, but they do a Merrie job of representing our collective id (that's the unconscious mind, bub). In fact, seven deadly sins just ain't enough to cover the failings and foibles of these terrors!

Leader of the gang
He may be supercool and always in control, but Bugs is no angel! At various times, the wabbit has been greedy, angry, gluttonous, lustful, proud, slothful... even envious (albeit of a turtle, his traditional fairy-tale enemy). It takes one debonair hare to look so good while being so bad.

Greed
When money, fame, or glory are up for grabs, you can count on Daffy Duck to do most of the grabbing! Driven by a despicable urge to get more than his fair share, Daffy makes no attempt to hide his greed. "Survival of the fittest," he says in *Rabbit Seasoning*, "and besides, it's fun!"

Anger
Yosemite Sam's downfall is his hair-trigger temper—the runty hombre will shoot you just for standing nearby.

Heavens above! Something about each one of the Looney Tunes touches our soul in ways we can all relate to.

Holier than thou

Cherub Elmer Fudd
Cherub Porky Pig

Elmer Fudd, Porky Pig, Tweety, Speedy Gonzales, and Road Runner: They act all innocent, but are they, really? Confidentially, Doc, there's a bit of bad in every good Looney Tune. On the rap sheet: shooting wabbits, choking d-d-darnfool ducks, making puddy tats go boom, dating everybody's "seester"... even just beep-beeping around you behind your back.

Envy

"Mars needs women" and "women come from Venus." Perhaps that's why Marvin the Martian envies Earthlings, who can see Venus directly. Marvin's view of this beautiful planet is blocked by our world, giving his failings Earth-shaking consequences for Bugs and Daffy.

Pride

"I'm Wile E. Coyote, supergenius!" Mix that ego with an Acme catalog and you've got a recipe for destruction (his own). The wily coyote's inflated self-worth leads his plans—and his gunpowder—to forever blow up in his face.

Gluttony

The Tasmanian Devil has a devil of an appetite! Cats, bats, dogs, hogs, elephants, antelopes, pheasants, ferrets, goats, and, especially, rabbits feature on his mega-menu. But the Devil's failure to look before he lunches has been his undoing—in the form of chef Bugs' TNT-laced Wild Turkey Surprise.

Lust

They say love is blind, and when Pepe Le Pew is in the grip of *l'amour*, he certainly loses sight of reality. One glimpse of a fetching female has the great skunk lover kissing his judgment goodbye and unknowingly pursuing... un cat!

Sloth

"I keep pitching 'em, and you keep missing 'em!" says Foghorn Leghorn to Henery Hawk. The laid-back rooster is too fast for the chicken hawk, but is otherwise a master of doing absolutely nothing.

You've got to give the devil his due, and Sylvester has had hell to pay more than once. In *Satan's Waitin'*, our puddy tat had nine lives to do things right—but still ended up sufferin' for his sins.

BUGS AND DAFFY

A SCREWY RABBIT and a darnfool duck. Debuting at a time when many cartoon stars were cute and innocuous, Bugs Bunny and Daffy Duck redefined animated humor with unprecedented intelligence and attitude. It's no wonder that the egomaniacal duck and unbeatable wild hare remain as fresh today as they have ever been.

BUGS BUNNY

HE'S SLY. HE'S SMART. He's witty. He's a screwball with attitude, a subtle verbal humorist with street savvy, and an American legend with no regard for scruples. He can croon like Bing, sing opera like Pagliacci— and he doesn't look bad in a dress, either! In short, Bugs is the zaniest and funniest performer in film history. No wonder we love him!

Bugs doesn't get out of bed for less than a crate of carrots, you know.

Hip hare
With his knowing glances at the audience and unflappable demeanor, Bugs is the undisputed king of cool.

"You know how I hate to talk about myself," claims humble Bugs in A Hare Grows In Manhattan—before launching into his life story.

Trademark schtick—Bugs shows his unshakeable composure by chomping casually on a carrot.

Celebrity status
Bugs is a Looney Tunes celebrity who always receives star billing in his cartoons. He is often cast in self-mythologizing roles which reveal his supposed biography. In *A Hare Grows in Manhattan* and others, he is interviewed at his opulent home in the style of a Hollywood actor, discussing his past as a poor bunny growing up on the East Side of New York City.

Bugs strikes a nonchalant pose in the Looney Tunes drum. He was also given his own logo that appeared at the opening credits.

American icon
Bugs is the most famous cartoon rabbit in the world and the internationally recognized symbol of Warner Bros. He often hops off the screen to appear in comic books and strips, and video games. Wabbit merchandise from cookie jars to boxer shorts sell like hot... carrot cakes!

Bugs has been called many things: wascally wabbit, long-eared varmint, "Brunhilde"— but in this comic book panel, he reveals his "real" name!

Bugs voluntarily steps into this rabbit trap in *Hare Remover*, not wanting to disappoint the numbskull who'd use a trap this obvious.

Pity for the enemy

Woe betide anyone foolish enough to consider hunting the brainy hare. Blowing Yosemite Sam's cool again and again in *Buccaneer Bunny* (right), Bugs declares at the finale, "I have not even begun to fight!" Whatever the threat, Bugs' composure is always complete, as he waits for his enemies to simply exhaust themselves. But for all Bugs' heckling, he also feels sympathy for his would-be assassins. They just picked on the wrong guy!

Bunny in disguise

Bugs' adversaries are usually huge, powerful, and heavily armed—our bunny star only has his wits and an extensive range of frocks! While his opponents single-mindedly pursue one object—capture of the rabbit—Bugs is free to amuse himself (and us) by play-acting a quick-fire succession of hilarious roles. The wisecracking hare seems to mock those who take themselves too seriously—and, by extension, the world.

The wabbit in another dandy disguise

Is Sam red-faced with rage—or is that just his mustache? Bugs versus the bandit in Hare Trimmed.

Acting up

Never underestimate our hero's ability to overact when the need arises. To get out of a corner, Bugs will fake his own death or convulse with mock terror. But his *piece de resistance* is to suddenly plant a big kiss on an opponent's lips! The rabbit's not shy when it comes to flouting social conventions.

Bugs is the pitcher and the catcher at the same time!

Rabbit for all seasons

Bugs combines superhuman street smarts and a head full of book learning. He's just as likely to single-handedly play every position on a major-league baseball team in *Baseball Bugs* (left) as kid around with classical concertos in *Rhapsody Rabbit* (right).

THE MANY SIDES OF BUGS!

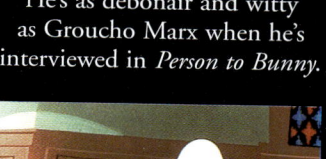

He's as debonair and witty as Groucho Marx when he's interviewed in *Person to Bunny*.

In *Bugs Bunny Rides Again*, he's determined—"Just like Gary Cooper, eh?"

He's as unflappable as Humphrey Bogart when he's held up in *Bonanza Bunny*.

He's as sassy and coy as Betty Grable when he waits on Hollywood stars in *Slick Hare*.

He's as pugnacious as James Cagney when he shows his muscles in *Rabbit Punch*.

SCREWBALL BUNNY

OUR FAVORITE LONG-EARED Looney Tune has outwitted hunters and adversaries using an seemingly inexhaustable range of tricks: He's bamboozled them with his irrepressible zaniness, talked rings around them with his wisecracking wit, and smothered them into submission with unexpected kisses. The bunny rules!

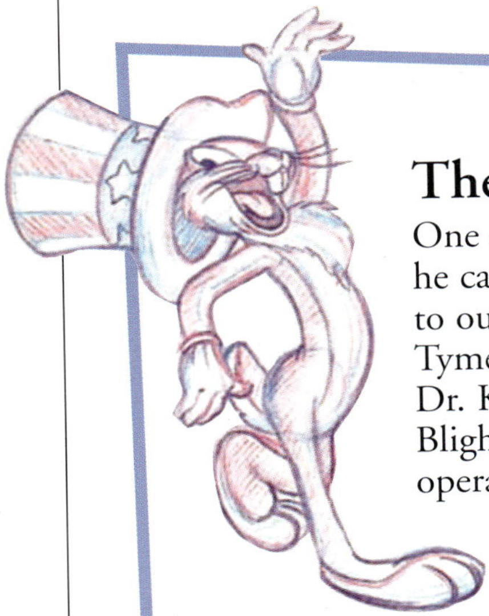

The trickster
One of Bugs' most endearing traits is that he can instantly become another personality to outwit his opponents. He's been Stychen Tyme, a tailor in *Bunny Hugged*, the quack Dr. Killpatient in *Hare Tonic*, bossy Captain Bligh in *Buccaneer Bunny*, and a slapstick operatic circus clown in *Acrobatty Bunny*.

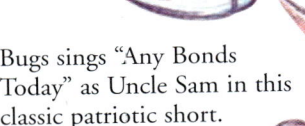

Bugs sings "Any Bonds Today" as Uncle Sam in this classic patriotic short.

Animator's pencil sketch of aged Bugs

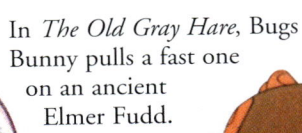

In *The Old Gray Hare*, Bugs Bunny pulls a fast one on an ancient Elmer Fudd.

Ehhh...
In Tex Avery's *A Wild Hare*, Bugs utters the lines "What's up, Doc?", creating in the process an immortal catchphrase. Voice artist Mel Blanc utilized a combination of Brooklyn and Bronx accents to give the character the perfect smart-aleck voice.

Rabbit roots
From Zomo the bunny in ancient Africa to Brer Rabbit in the American South, people have always hailed tales of oppressed forest friends getting even. So when Bugs emerged as a heckling heir to those far-off fables, the world was watching. When he established himself in a class above his fictional forebears, we started cheering. And we've never stopped.

Uncanny powers
So convincing is Bugs' scary impersonations of "the horrible Frankincense monster" in *Hare Conditioned* that the rabbit frightens himself out of his wits—when he only intended to ward off a pesky department store manager!

In *What's Cookin' Doc?*, Bugs campaigns for an Oscar using his "Edward G. Robinson" impersonation.

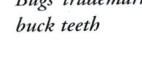
Bugs' trademark buck teeth

Only dapper rabbits wear white gloves.

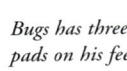
Bugs has three pads on his feet.

King of cool

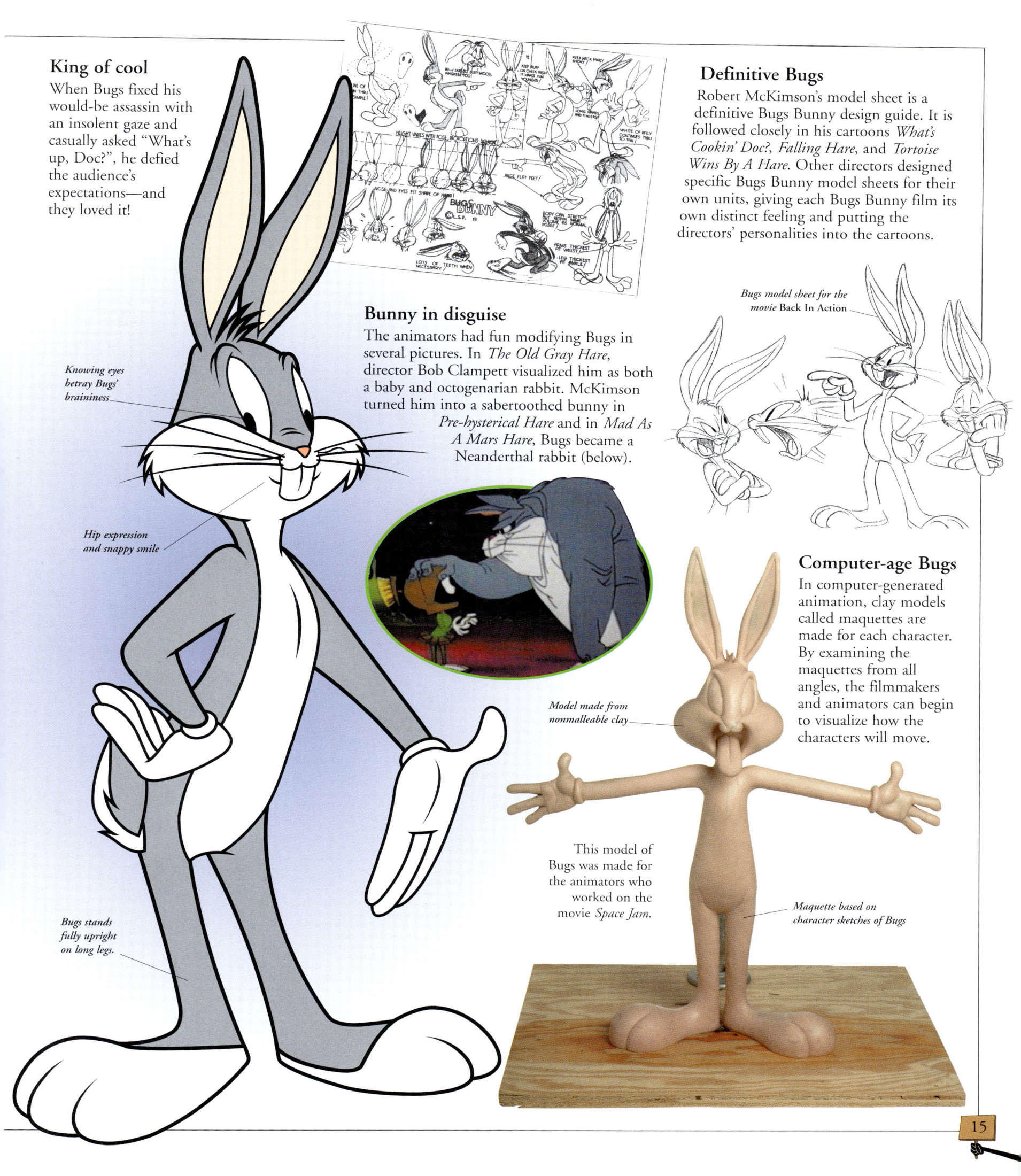

When Bugs fixed his would-be assassin with an insolent gaze and casually asked "What's up, Doc?", he defied the audience's expectations—and they loved it!

Knowing eyes betray Bugs' braininess

Hip expression and snappy smile

Bugs stands fully upright on long legs.

Definitive Bugs

Robert McKimson's model sheet is a definitive Bugs Bunny design guide. It is followed closely in his cartoons *What's Cookin' Doc?*, *Falling Hare*, and *Tortoise Wins By A Hare*. Other directors designed specific Bugs Bunny model sheets for their own units, giving each Bugs Bunny film its own distinct feeling and putting the directors' personalities into the cartoons.

Bugs model sheet for the movie Back In Action

Bunny in disguise

The animators had fun modifying Bugs in several pictures. In *The Old Gray Hare*, director Bob Clampett visualized him as both a baby and octogenarian rabbit. McKimson turned him into a sabertoothed bunny in *Pre-hysterical Hare* and in *Mad As A Mars Hare*, Bugs became a Neanderthal rabbit (below).

Computer-age Bugs

In computer-generated animation, clay models called maquettes are made for each character. By examining the maquettes from all angles, the filmmakers and animators can begin to visualize how the characters will move.

Model made from nonmalleable clay

This model of Bugs was made for the animators who worked on the movie *Space Jam*.

Maquette based on character sketches of Bugs

BUGS' BURROW

Home sweet home
Home is often any place Bugs can hang his long ears. But his preferred and most common habitat tends to be in the forest hills behind Elmer Fudd's suburban neighborhood.

Daisy Lou—Bugs' part-time date and a source of drag clothing

Custom midnight snack shelf

Carrot patch-pattern bedspread

Duck disguise from Duck! Rabbit! Duck!

King's crown from Rabbit Hood

Brunhilde costume from What's Opera, Doc?

Sweater, to fool opera singers into giving explosive autographs (from Long-Haired Hare*)*

Carmen Miranda headdress from What's Cookin' Doc?

Fox costume from Foxy By Proxy

Wards off wolves in grandma's clothing

Secret exit for Bugs to make a quick getaway or for guests without climbing skills

Bunny bed
Average rabbits snooze in a pile of grass. Bugs Bunny, being a most sophisticated member of his species, prefers a four-poster feather bed. It's as soft and sensitive as its owner, leading to seismic shakeups when visitors walk over the ceiling (as here, when the circus comes to town in *Acrobatty Bunny*).

I**F A MAN'S HOME** is his castle, Bugs Bunny's hole in the ground is a subterranean palace designed for a gentleman rabbit's comfort. Every nook is filled with the latest rabbit-friendly utilities, including high-tech carrot juicers and, of course, hare-conditioning. Every cranny reflects the special needs of a brainy, cultured bunny with plenty of no-goods to battle and a great deal of pranks to be played. C'mon, step inside—and have a carrot!

Bugs' friends and friendly rivals often drop by for an evening of T.V. on the rabbit's big screen. Here's Daffy enjoying *Scooby Doo*.

BUGS IN DRAG

IN THE 1992 MOVIE *Wayne's World*, Garth Algar (Dana Carvey) asks the question, "Did you ever find Bugs Bunny attractive when he put on a dress and played a girl bunny?" His buddy Wayne didn't, but Elmer Fudd, Yosemite Sam, and the Tasmanian Devil are just a few of the many males who have been bewitched, bothered, and bewildered by Bugs' seemingly endless wardrobe of women's clothing.

In Bob Clampett's *Bugs Bunny Gets The Boid*, flirtatious Bugs sports long eyelashes, lipstick, a showercap, and a towel to tease Beaky Buzzard. "You naughty, naughty boy!" scolds the wacky wabbit.

Dressed to thrill

Bugs' cross-dressing has provoked much discussion and speculation. The Warner Bros. animators were, no doubt, influenced by silent movies and vaudeville comedy routines in which male characters dressed up in women's clothing to elude pursuers. It certainly gives Bugs the psychological advantage over his foes, dazzling them with his unnerving self-confidence. It also helps Bugs get in touch with his feminine side!

The unlikely couple

Bugs appears in drag in The Wabbit Who Came To Supper.

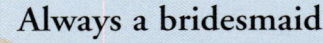

Original pencil animation from Hare Trimmed

Always a bridesmaid

Bugs' female guises have led him close to tying the knot on a few occasions. In *Hare Trimmed*, he tries to outwit Yosemite Sam, who's out to marry Granny and bilk her out of her fortune. Bugs disguises himself as the old lady, ultimately leading Sam down the aisle himself! A torn wedding dress ends the charade. "Boo-hoo," Bugs laments. "Always a bridesmaid!"

Lady Taz

Pretending to be a Tasmanian Devil's love interest in *Bedevilled Rabbit*, Bugs loads a steel bear trap in his mouth to give Taz a special smack on the lips. Taz is smitten—and bitten—by Bugs' lip lock. When Taz is finally hauled away by his jealous She-Devil, the bunny is quite gracious. Says Bugs, "She's a nice lady... Ewwww!"

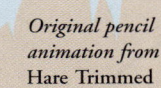

With his blonde locks and harp, Lorelei the mermaid is one of Bugs' most alluring impersonations. In *Hare Ribbin'*, he leads a hunting dog underwater for an extended chase in a lake. There he plays "tag" with the pooch, knocking him through a sea wall with his large tail fin.

Wild in the country
Bugs outwits two feuding bumpkins in Robert McKimson's *Hillbilly Hare* by donning a rural "Daisy-Mae" outfit that has them going ga-ga. Bugs' square dance with brothers Curt and Pumpkinhead Martin leads to a slapstick sequence which is one of the funniest pieces of musical mayhem ever created.

Totally befuddled
Bugs employs one of his most elaborate female ensembles in Chuck Jones' *Rabbit Seasoning*. Elmer Fudd is instantly smitten and quickly seduced by Bugs' Lana Turner turn into blasting Daffy Duck once more.

Tutti-fruity booby
Brazilian bombshell Carmen Miranda was caricatured in several cartoons such as *Slick Hare* and *Hollywood Canine Canteen*. In Bob Clampett's *What's Cookin' Doc?*, Bugs tries to woo the Motion Picture Academy into giving him an Oscar with his Miranda impersonation, but all he wins is the "Booby Prize Oscar."

Bugs' Granny is an effective disguise.

Original animation drawing from What's Cookin' Doc?

The look of love!

Bugs plants a good one on the hare-baiting senator in Rebel Rabbit.

One of the boldest weapons in Bugs comic arsenal is the "wacky kiss" he plants on his foes, which usually renders them speechless. Well, what would *you* do if your enemy suddenly gave you big smack on the lips? It takes all the fight out of you, doesn't it!

HERE COMES TROUBLE

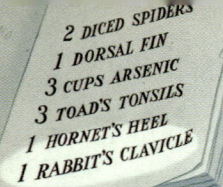

BUGS BUNNY has encountered a large share of troublemakers who never fail to underestimate his abilities. Chuck Jones established the golden rule: "Bugs must always be provoked." The rabbit never initiates conflict, but when pushed... he gives *worse* than he gets!

The Easter Rabbit
In *Easter Yeggs*, a sad-sack Easter Rabbit recruits Bugs to deliver a basket of "technicolor hen fruit" to two of his worst clients—a little brat with a hammer and Elmer Fudd trying to catch some "Easter wabbit stew." Guess which characters get egg on their faces?

Bugs is served a drugged carrot in Bewitched Bunny

Witch Hazel
This crazy cackling witch, voiced by June Foray, prides herself on her ugliness. In *Broom-Stick Bunny*, trick-or-treating Bugs challenges her supreme ugliness with his disguise. He saves Hansel and Gretel from her cooking pot in *Bewitched Bunny* and gets chased around Macbeth's castle in *A Witch's Tangled Hare*.

When Bugs hits gold ore (with his head) in *Barbary-Coast Bunny*, he is immediately suckered out of it by the villainous Nasty Canasta. Canasta uses the bunny's treasure to build a casino but, as Bugs reminds us, "You realize this is not going to go unchallenged."

Witch Hazel's haunted house

The bull was one of Bugs' fiercest opponents. Chuck Jones had no intention of making bullfighting the subject of a cartoon until the day when, out of the blue, producer Eddie Selzer instructed him not to make bullfighting films. "So I made *Bully For Bugs*," recalled Jones, "not because I was interested in bullfighting particularly, but because he said not to."

Pencil sketch of Mrs. Gorilla

Gorillas
Robert McKimson introduced Mrs. Gorilla and her henpecked husband, Gruesome, in *Gorilla My Dreams*. When Bugs agrees to be their child, Gruesome is less than thrilled. Papa gorilla ends up knocking himself out by chasing "junior" through the jungle. He gets another pounding in the follow-up, *Apes of Wrath*.

"Whomp your partner with all your might...."

Double trouble
When Bugs sees double, he knows it's trouble. Curt and Pumpkinhead Martin are a pair of twisted mountain men in *Hillbilly Hare*. The wabbit outsmarts the pair by calling a hilarious square dance, forcing them to pull beards, whomp each other with fence posts and wallow in the pig pen.

Witch Hazel has always had a thing for Bugs Bunny. "You look like Paul—my pet tarantula," she pines.

"Don't they look yummy-yummy?"

What's cooking?
In *French Rarebit*, set in Paris, twin chefs Francois and Louie fight over the bunny's secret recipe for "Louisiana Bayou Backbay Bunny Borderlay, à la Antoine." This requires both cooks to become stand-in rabbits and be broiled in oil. C'est magnifique!

In *Hyde and Hare*, Bugs convinces Dr. Jekyll to adopt him—not realizing he has a little secret....

BAD TO WORSE!

Nero Lion receives a lesson in circus etiquette from Bugs in *Acrobatty Bunny*.

Bugs convinces the Snowman that Daffy Duck is *The Abominable Snow Rabbit*.

A Mohican aims to give Bugs a "hare cut and scalp treatment" in *A Feather In His Hare*.

The Big Bad Wolf tries to outsmart Bugs in *Now, Hare This* and *False Hare*.

Here's where this book *really* begins!

21

TRULY DAFFY

DAFFY DUCK was the first character to truly personify Warner Bros.' madcap humor. In his early cartoons, he is totally deranged: bouncing off the walls, singing "Merry-Go-Round Broke Down" (the Looney Tunes title music), and driving Hollywood directors crazy—silly, surreal, and hilarious. Altogether now: "Woo-hoo-hoo!"

Daffy stole the show in Tex Avery's cartoon, Porky's Duck Hunt.

"¡OOH ¡OOM"

First appearance
Daffy began life as what Chuck Jones called a "wild and unrestrained screwy duck." In *Porky's Duck Hunt*, Daffy bounces across a marsh, laughing hysterically at the pudgy pig and his dog (here named Rin-Tin-Tin) until the frustrated pig points out a move that isn't in the script. The duck simply replies, "I'm just a crazy darn-fool duck." And how!

Original pencil animation from Porky's Duck Hunt

True original
Daffy Duck was the first cartoon character to be named after a state of utter lunacy, predating "Bugs" Bunny and the "Goofy" Gophers. Daffy was also unique in that he had no reason to be so manic—he just was! Each director found ways to develop the duck's character, adding something new to the mix and making him increasingly complex.

Big star
Daffy's rise to stardom was meteoric. "People weren't accustomed to seeing a cartoon character do these things," said director Bob Clampett. "People would leave the theaters talking about this daffy duck."

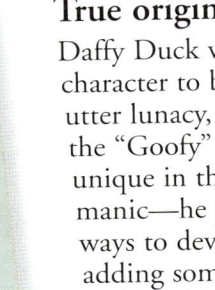
Daffy and Porky appear on an animator's model sheet.

This is what happens when you get stuck in an artificial lung.

Porky's pal
In his early pairings with Porky, Daffy played the clown to the stuttering pig's straight man. In *Porky And Daffy* (right) the pig assists as the slap-happy duck's boxing manager. As *The Daffy Doc* (above), the duck plucks a perfectly healthy Porky off the street and chases him around a madcap medical center. They end up falling through an artificial lung, which causes each of their body parts to inflate in turn.

Aspiring star Daffy won't let movie producer I.M. Stupendous say no in Daffy Duck In Hollywood.

Two nuts together

Daffy's appearance in *Daffy Duck And Egghead* is his all-time craziest. In the opening titles, two "nuts" emerge from walnut shells—Daffy and Egghead, the human hunter who will become Elmer Fudd. Director Tex Avery gives the hunter a classic gag that breaks the fourth wall: Egghead shoots a guy in the audience who won't sit down! At the end, the men (actually, the ducks) in the white coats take Daffy away.

Dr. I.C. Spots: CASE NOTES
DAFFY DUCK

As you will see on the next few pages, Mr. Daffy Duck is one of the strangest cases of split personality I have ever encountered. He evolved from one neurosis to another—from a raving lunatic to a selfish, egotistical scoundrel, with delusions of grandeur. I have monitored his actions very closely and I'm sure you will agree: This one's for the birds!

In Robert McKimson's *Daffy Doodles*, Daffy plays the part of the "mustache maniac." He paints mustaches on billboards, subway riders, and irate policemen (including Porky) all over the city. Then, when he is taken to court, he is found "not guilty"—by a mustachioed jury!

Henpecked quack
The flip side to Daffy's lunacy is his role as a troubled married man and father. In *The Henpecked Duck* (right), Daffy's wife wants to divorce him for losing her eggs while practicing a magic disappearing trick.

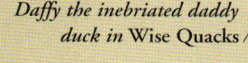

Daffy the inebriated daddy duck in Wise Quacks

Cross-eyed and madcap!

Daffy traits
Jumping, spinning, and shouting "woo-hoo-hoo"—these are the trademarks of the early, Looney Tuney Daffy Duck. Other common traits include a cross-eyed glaze, gobs of spit emitted when talking, and offering to read the bumps on people's heads (after creating the bumps first).

Pressed duck

HIS BITTER HALF

DAFFY DUCK has always had a strong will to succeed, expressed in a hyperactive but essentially carefree way. At his most extreme, however, this competitive streak turns the duck into a vulture consumed by envy, greed, and an ego the size of Pennsylvania. Yet, his pathological need to be the biggest star provides some of his biggest laughs.

In *Person To Bunny*, Daffy is desperate to be noticed. Either that or he believes his arm is a necktie.

Daffy is prepared to fry for his art.

Character portrait

When this animators' character sheet was produced, Daffy Duck was often completely bonkers, wacko, touched, oofti-ma-goofti. In medical terms, he was suffering from acute *Texius Averius* with a distinct touch of *Clampetitus*.

Notice Daffy's proclivity toward violence.

Rabbit envy

One of the reasons Daffy has apparently let his dark side come to light is this rabbit. Heck hath no fury like a duck scorned. Or is that scorched? Oh, well, it doesn't matter. He's jealous of the rabbit's adoring fans. He's jealous of the rabbit's cool demeanor. He's even jealous of the rabbit's ears.

Daffy's after big cash prizes again in The Million Hare's TV gameshow.

ADDITIONAL CASE NOTES ON DAFFY BY DR. I.C. SPOTS

1. Patient has hair-trigger temper.
2. Patient is a serial user of mallets, firearms, and explosives.
3. Find new patient.

The price of fame

Daffy feels he must be first at any cost. His competitive nature has cost him several broken limbs and a bruised ego. Not to mention the occasional bullet through the head—witness the shot fired by Daffy himself in *The Scarlet Pumpernickel* to show the studio bigwigs he means business!

"It's getting so you have to kill yourself to sell a story 'round here," complains Daffy in *The Scarlet Pumpernickel*.

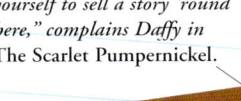

"MINE! MINE! MINE!"

Hot air coming out of mouth is good for doctor's arthritis.

Stars in his eyes

Daffy's twin obsessions—desire for fame and love of money—are combined in Robert McKimson's *People Are Bunny*, in which the duck spots a TV hunting show giving out big prizes for captured rabbits. However, when the show abruptly switches to duck season, guess who ends up getting blasted?

Daffy hunting for trouble

In *A Star Is Bored*, devious Daffy enters a world of pain when he accepts the job of movie stuntman on the latest Bugs Bunny star vehicle in the vain belief that he'll steal every scene.

Fame, fatal fame

Daffy seems to want to be in show business in the worst way—which is exactly the way he's in it.
In *Person To Bunny*, he becomes fixated on being able to perform his act on TV, but, when faced with an audience of 40 million, the duck lets his insecurity get the better of him—and ducks out!

Daffy asserts his need for control on a befuddled Fudd, telling him to "never darken my floor again."

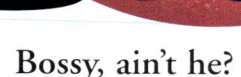

Bossy, ain't he?

Daffy tends to order people around as if they were waiters in his personal café. He's so bad, when he looks in the mirror, he orders his reflection to shape up! At one time in his life, he acted henpecked. So now, he might be overcompensating. Or, he might just be a big jerk. Whatever.

"I'm rich, I'm wealthy—yahoo! I'm comfortably well-off."

Even when magically turned into an oyster-sized duck, greedy Daffy just won't "clam up."

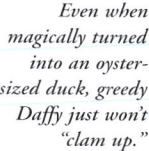

Greedy duck

In *Ali Baba Bunny*, the sight of a humungous pile of treasure produces a range of responses in Daffy: first, an enraptured trance, followed by the evil glare of pure greed, and, finally, an uncontrollable mania as he attempts to lay claim to the fortune and readjust to his newfound wealth. Challenged by Bugs, who shows not the remotest interest in even the tiniest diamond in the pile, Daffy rationally explains: "I can't help it. I'm a greedy slob. It's my hobby."

Daffy Duck: psychiatric profile

Feathered alter egos
Fearless, self-assured, and all-knowing—or so he thinks! Daffy Duck has taken on roles that demand brains, brawn, and bravery, while his vivid imagination allows him to mimic the greatest heroes of the screen. If imitation is the sincerest form of flattery, then this duck has buttered-up the greatest literary characters ever created—and his hilarious misadventures have made for some of the funniest Warner Bros. cartoons.

Duck in space
The greatest of Daffy's fantasies is his sci-fi adventure in *Duck Dodgers in the 24 1/2th Century*. This Chuck Jones cartoon was inspired by Buck Rogers, a space hero of comic strips and movie serials in the 1920s and 30s. Dodgers and his Eager Young Space Cadet (Porky Pig) battle Marvin the Martian for control of Planet X, source of the last-remaining supply of aludium fozdex, the shaving cream atom. A battle of nit-wits ensues.

After Marvin the Martian obliterates Duck Dodgers with his disintegrator weapon, space cadet Porky uses his Integrating Pistol to revive the dazed duck.

Layout sketch

Duck Twacy about to get rubbed out by the dastardly villain, Rubber Head!

Swashbuckling Daffy as the Scarlet Pumpernickel.

Stupor Duck is the alter ego of Cluck Trent!

Detectives and highwaymen
"Nothing's impossible to Duck Twacy!" Daffy's admiration of the famous newspaper comic-strip detective Dick Tracy leads him to an entire fantasy adventure as "Duck Twacy" in Bob Clampett's *The Great Piggy Bank Robbery*. Daffy's fantasy life hits overload in *The Scarlet Pumpernickel*, when he tries to persuade studio bosses to make a "serious" movie with himself as a daring young highwayman.

Stupor Duck
In Robert McKimson's *Stupor Duck*, Daffy is a mild mannered reporter who eavesdrops on the diabolical threats of Aardvark Ratnik coming from his editor's office. Those threats, however, are from a television drama, and the mistaken Stupor Duck flies off to confront the fictional Ratnik—his beak receiving the majority of the smashing.

Unfortunately for Duck Dodgers, when he pulls the trigger on his Disintegrating Pistol, the gun itself disappears!

Original background painting

Daffy's other alter egos:
Detective Duck Drake—private eye, ear, nose, and throat
Dorlock Holmes—the British detective
Friar Duck—from Merrie England
...etc, etc.

DAFFY'S DELUSIONS

WITH HIS SUPREME confidence and massive ego, Daffy truly believes he can be anybody he wants to be and do extraordinary deeds. And wherever he finds himself—the Old West, outer space, or in the deep recesses of his own mind—the duck has stared squarely at danger, laughed in the face of jeopardy, looked chaos straight in the eyes—and had his beak blown off!

False rabbit ears (worn in Duck Season)

Daffy wants nothing more than the fame and glory awarded to Bugs Bunny. After all, he's smarter, more talented, and more popular than the rabbit—of course he is!

The Masked Avenger
As a cowboy in Chuck Jones' *Dripalong Daffy*, Daffy vows to clean up "this one-horse town." That means standing up to rustler, bandit, and square-dance caller, Nasty Canasta, who quickly subdues the duck with a shot of his "usual" saloon drink—a stiff drink that literally stiffens the drinker!

The return of Dripalong
In Chuck Jones' *My Little Duckaroo*, Daffy as the Masked Avenger goes up against Canasta again, with Porky Pig as his grizzled, comic sidekick. Of course, it's Porky who brings down the bad guy and becomes the true hero—much to the duck's frustration.

Daffy dressed as Bugs when he tried to sabotage The Bugs Bunny Show.

Duck meets duck
In *Duck Amuck*, Daffy becomes a musketeer, a pilot, a sailor, and a farmer. He is also erased, colored blue, and transformed into a flower headed, four-legged creature! In this film, Daffy is aware of being a cartoon character and he puts up with a lot of abuse from the paintbrush of his animator before demanding to know who's in charge. He never finds out that it was Bugs Bunny—who slyly admits, "Ain't I a stinker?"

Duck Amuck is a Chuck Jones masterpiece—and a revealing look inside the tortured mind of Daffy Duck!

Bunny heels attract stray, snap-happy sheepdogs.

"Yoiks! And away!" In *Robin Hood Daffy*, the duck never quite manages to convince Friar Porky of his true identity.

DAFFY VS. BUGS

"KEEP YOUR FRIENDS CLOSE, but your enemies closer," advises Michael Corleone in *The Godfather Part 2*, a viewpoint to which Daffy Duck appears to subscribe. At one time a great admirer of Bugs Bunny, the duck evolved into a frustrated rival. When he and Bugs team up—most often for hunting season, show-business goings-on, or far-flung adventures—Daffy's manic desire to outdo Bugs reaches truly disturbing proportions.

Remember...
1. *If you're looking for fun*
2. *You don't need a reason*
3. *All you need is a gun*
4. *It's Rabbit Season!*

Bugs Bunny's winter home is in the California desert.

In *Rabbit Fire*, Daffy and Bugs put Elmer off the scent with a couple of hasty impressions. Daffy quacks "What's up, Doc?" while Bugs just puts on a lisp.

Hunting season
Chuck Jones directed a trilogy of hunting cartoons featuring Bugs, Daffy, and Elmer: *Rabbit Fire*, *Rabbit Seasoning*, and *Duck! Rabbit! Duck!* Bugs' confusing wordplay and Fudd's stubborn hunting logic lead the trio into dizzy debates over whether it's rabbit season, duck season, baseball season—or whether Fudd's got a "fricasseeing rabbit" license. As the loser is always Daffy, the duck has determined one thing about Bugs: he's "despicable!"

Beak geek
In *Rabbit Fire*, Daffy and Bugs try everything they can think of to persuade the befuddled hunter to shoot the other one. Bugs easily outwits Daffy, and the result is always the same: the duck's beak is blown off in every possible (and impossible) direction!

Recipes for disaster
In *Rabbit Fire*, Daffy and Bugs swap recipe ideas to persuade Elmer of the other's superior taste. On the menu: Duck polonaise under glass ("umm-um!"); rabbit au gratin de gelatin under tubed leather ("drool, drool!"); barbecued duck meat with broiled duck bill Milanese ("yummy-yum!"); chicken fried rabbit with cottontail sauce, braised in carrots! Too bad Fudd's a vegetarian.

Daffy with deranged jealousy on his mind

Blueprint from the Acme Corporation

Operation Rabbit
(Or "reasons for loathing Bugs")

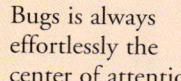
Bugs is always effortlessly the center of attention.

In *Duck Amuck*, Bugs has the power to make Daffy ski through the desert.

Bugs Bunny receives more column inches for his feature-film appearances than Daffy—or so the jealous duck believes.

Bugs and his "booby prize" Oscar from *What's Cookin', Doc?*

Wrong turns at Albuquerque
As travel companions, Bugs and Daffy get lost in the strangest places, providing ample opportunity for the duck to cash in—and the bunny to outwit. In ancient Baghdad, the duck is bedeviled by cave guardian Hassan and an evil genie of the lamp; in the Himalayan Mountains, they outrun the Abominable Snowman; and at the top of the beanstalk, Daffy "Jack" and Bugs elude a giant-sized Elmer Fudd.

Daffy lets stage magician Bugs saw him in half in *Show Biz Bugs*, intending to show the audience what a charlatan the hare is. As ever, though, the duck gets unstuck....

Show biz rivals
Daffy is especially jealous of Bugs' show biz fame. In cartoons such as *A Star Is Bored*, Daffy loses his cool as Bugs' stand-in. On television shows such as *People Are Bunny*, *Person To Bunny*, *The Million Hare*, and *The Bugs Bunny Show*, the duck tries to upstage the wabbit's close-ups. But their professional rivalry reaches its peak on the stage in *Show Biz Bugs*, wherein Daffy's jealousy causes him to do his ultimate, explosive stage act. Says the departing duck: "I can only do it once!"

Duck wars
Although Bugs is the prime target on Daffy's twisted mind, the duck has also waged war against Porky Pig, Elmer Fudd, Foghorn Leghorn, Taz, Speedy, and the Goofy Gophers.

The battle of wills in *Show Biz Bugs* climaxes with Daffy determined to show up his rival. "First I drink a generous portion of gasoline, then some nitro glycerine, a goodly amount of gun powder, some Uranium 2-38. Shake well. Strike an ordinary match...". The results are explosive!

The final straw for Daffy's bruised ego!

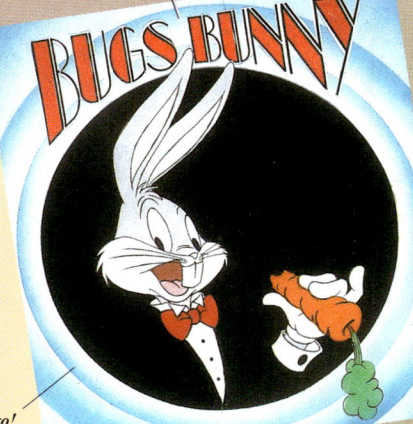

THE COMPANY

WARNER BROS. spawned more star cartoon characters than any other animation studio. Porky, Elmer, Yosemite Sam, and the others form a company of actors who play a variety of roles on the Looney Tunes stage. They are truly an all-star team, filled with strong personalities, outrageous attitudes, and big laughs.

P-P-PORKY PIG

WITH HIS ENDEARING stutter and never-say-die attitude, Porky Pig always wins over the audience. Who would have thought that a shy pig with a speech impediment would become a cartoon s-s-s-superstar? Perhaps the secret of his success is his engaging character, with its mix of humor and pathos, making the audience laugh at his predicament while weeping at his embarrassment. Looney Tunes' very own "everypig" has always stood out from the crowd!

The looney gang
In Friz Freleng's *I Haven't Got A Hat*, Porky is one of a group of animal schoolkids inspired by Hal Roach's live action Our Gang series. At first, the animators thought that Beans would be the new star....

Model sheet from I Haven't Got A Hat

OLIVER OWL — HAM AND EX — BEANS — TOMMY TURTLE — KITTY — PORKY

One of the gang
The Looney Tunes "gang" included Porky, wise-guy Beans the cat, mischievous twin puppies, Ham and Ex, know-it-all Oliver Owl, Tommy Turtle, and Little Kitty, a girl cat. Some of the characters only appeared briefly; others, like Beans, featured in a few cartoons, but Porky was the one to capture the audiences' hearts. He had that special something: star quality!

Porky Pig and Beans the cat are classmates in *I Haven't Got A Hat*.

Performing pups Ham and Ex.

Nervous Kitty attempts to sing "Mary Had A Little Lamb."

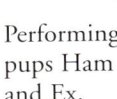 ### Beans the cat
Beans and Porky made a contrasting pair: the first a confident cat, the second a timid pig. The cartoons in which they appeared together took comic absurdity and slapstick to new levels. In Tex Avery's *Gold Diggers of '49*, Beans discovers gold and lets the whole town know, which leads to a frantic car chase featuring Beans and Porky.

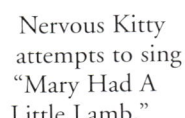 ### Stuttering star
Porky' stutter gives him trouble as he tries to recite the poem "Paul Revere's Ride" by Longfellow in *I Haven't Got A Hat*. The stutter was the one thing about Porky that never changed. Porky was originally voiced by Joe Dougherty, a real stammerer who proved to be too expensive—his recording sessions took hours! Replacement Mel Blanc added a comic edge to the dialog, using the stammer to create a classic comic personality.

Porky and Daffy

Porky was a perfect straight man to screwball Daffy Duck. He was boxing manager to Daffy the fighter in *Porky and Daffy* (right) and a patient to Daffy's crazed surgeon in *The Daffy Doc*. In *You Ought To Be In Pictures*, they cause havoc on the studio set.

Porky has played a variety of roles, appearing both as a boy and as an adult. Films such as *Wholly Smoke*, where Porky is a youngster, were made alongside such classics as *Porky's Romance*, in which he proposes marriage to his girlfriend Petunia.

Porky knows the best way to revive his fighter—and it involves a metal pan and Daffy's head.

A model sheet for Porky Pig.

In Porky and Gabby, *a camping trip becomes a series of madcap mishaps.*

Porky sometimes appeared with quick-tempered Gabby Goat, who had a talent for getting Porky into dangerous situations.

Pig tales

Porky Pig appeared in a great variety of adventure scenarios. He battled the Gorgon in ancient Greece and fought ghosts in a haunted house; he explored Egypt, joined the Navy and the Foreign Legion, and flew to surreal Wackyland. He has also been cast as a giant-killer and a pied piper. Whatever the setting, Porky coped in his usual resolute style.

Porky signs up for Air Corps. duty in *Plane Dippy*.

Our favorite pig stands tall in a scene from *Porky In Wackyland*.

"That's all folks!"

Warner Bros. cartoons traditionally ended with the lead character saying "That's all folks." When Porky broke through a drum to stammer the famous line, it went on to become an enduring trademark of Looney Tunes.

B-B-BIG DEAL!

AFTER YEARS as a Looney Tunes icon and Warner Bros. top cartoon star, Porky began to be eclipsed in popularity by the brasher characters Daffy Duck and Bugs Bunny. But the pig's career was far from over. He proved to be just as hilarious in supporting parts as he was in starring roles—proving he *was* a b-b-big deal!

Live-action landmark
Friz Freleng briefly left the Schlesinger studio to work at the lavish MGM studio on their bigger budgeted cartoons, but soon returned. His first film back home, *You Ought To Be In Pictures*, brilliantly combined live action and animation, predating *Space Jam* and *Back In Action*.

This landmark film featured Porky and Schlesinger himself!

Porky is perpetualy peturbed!

You Ought To Be In Pictures
In the film, Daffy talks his rival Porky into leaving the Looney Tunes studio and trying his luck in feature films. But it all goes terribly wrong, and the pig returns to discover that the scheming Daffy wanted him out of the way so that he could persuade Leon Schlesinger to make him the star of the show.

Real-life people who appear in the film include writer Michael Maltese (as a studio guard who chases Porky), executive Henry Binder, animator Gerry Chiniquy, and checker Gladys Hallberg. Mel Blanc provided all the voices except Schlesinger's.

You Ought To Be In Pictures contains rare scenes at the original Warner Bros. lot.

A pig's progress
Kids loved Porky, and his licensed merchandise was hugely successful. But as audiences became more sophisticated, the character was changed to suit their tastes. Michael Maltese said, "We made him into a grownup, teamed him with Daffy once in a while, and we gave him more grownup stories."

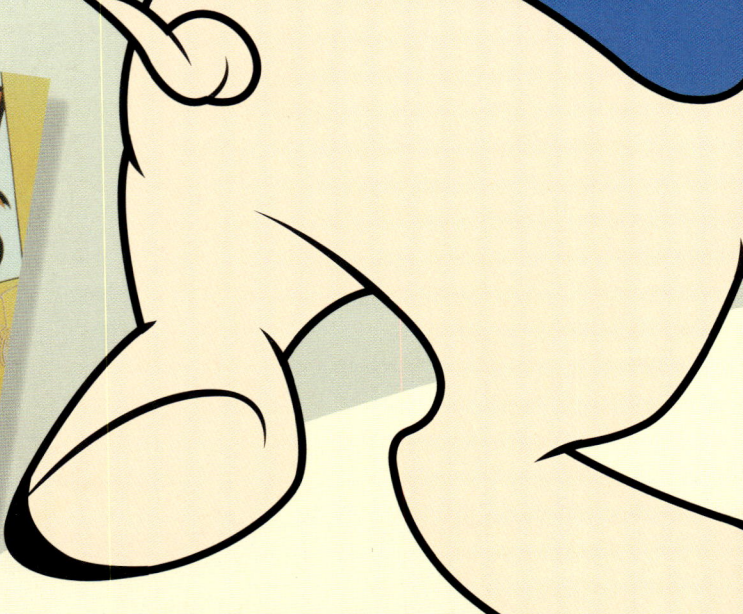

Porky's pets

Although Porky has had plenty of pets, he hasn't had much luck with them! In *Porky's Party*, his dog Black Fury goes crazy and shaves himself. Flat Foot Flooky, his pet pooch in *Porky's Tire Trouble*, tumbles into a vat of rubberizing solution. Porky's most famous pet, however, was Sylvester. The "Scaredy Cat" appeared in three cartoons in which he frantically tried to convince Porky of such unlikely sounding (but very real) threats as murderous mice or invading aliens!

Porky comics

Porky was star of the original Looney Tunes and Merrie Melodies comics, and before long he was given his own all-Porky comic books. His main artist was Roger Armstrong, who drew the pig for decades, but occasionally other artists would guest. One distinguished guest writer-artist, the legendary Carl Barks, created "Porky of the Mounties" (in Four Color #48). An original copy of Barks' Porky epic now fetches well over $1,000 on the collectors market!

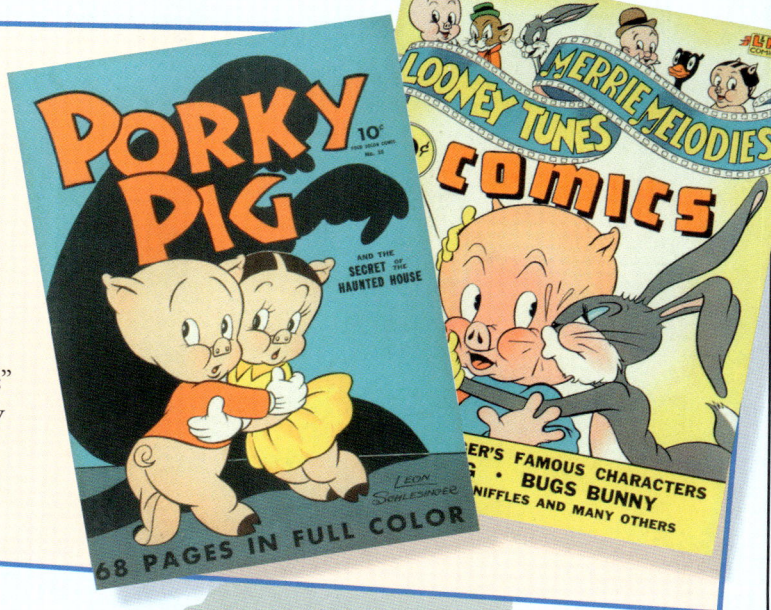

Porky has little patience with Sylvester's far-fetched-sounding stories.

Porky chops

Bob Clampett and Chuck Jones both helped to turn the overstuffed porker of the early cartoons into a more appealing character. Clampett made him a boy scout who always kept his cool in the midst of chaos, such as when running a baby delivery service with Daffy in *Baby Bottleneck*. Jones' Porky was either a fusspot (in films with Sylvester or Charlie Dog) or a cynic (as sidekick to Daffy Duck). Of the latter, Jones stated, "Porky is the observer, stating what the audience is thinking." Perhaps that's the secret of the pig's popularity—the audience feels that he's one of them.

Though Porky is known in the U.S. for his stutter, when dubbed into foreign languages his voice is often sans stutter, with perfect elocution!

Petunia Pig

Petunia appeared in *Porky's Romance* and *Porky's Double Trouble* as a golddigger who wrapped poor Porky around her finger. Bob Clampett made her cuter and altogether more attractive for her later roles, but it was as Porky's sweetheart in Looney Tunes comics and merchandising that she was most successful.

Petunia was voiced by Shirley Reed.

Space Cadet

Porky's best-known latter-day role was as Duck Dodgers' "Eager Young Space Cadet." His calm reactions to Dodgers' manic ramblings were as endearing as they were funny. The stammering Space Cadet's naive charm pleasantly redefined the Pig's personality, giving him a persona that endures today in the new Duck Dodgers TV series.

ELMER FUDD

THE WORLD'S MOST FAMOUS huntsman cuts an unforgettable image. Sneaking into the woods with his toddler physique, ill-fitting hunting gear, and a smile that's half-sly, half-stupid, Elmer J. Fudd is a simpleton with a shotgun. And if Elmer's looks don't make it clear enough, his voice is the clincher: He's vewy, vewy silly. *Heh-heh-heh-heh-heh.*

Fuddese gwammar was so popuwar that diwectors utiwized it themsewves.

Early Fudd
Fudd's earliest screen roles included solo comic turns and stardom in film parodies (*Confederate Honey*, for example, was based on *Gone With The Wind*). But the twend didn't wast and Elmer came to be exclusively defined as a duck and bunny foe.

"WABBIT TWACKS!"

Citizen Fudd
Predator and prey most often meet during the hunt. But Bugs bothers Elmer in all walks of life. In *The Unruly Hare*, the bunny pesters Fudd as a railroad surveyor, while in *Elmer's Pet Rabbit* (left) he invades his master's suburban home to dance, battle... and shower!

100 percent insuwated, waterpwoof, high-gwade boots

Fudd voiceman Arthur Q. Bryan lent his memorable tones to this and other classic children's recordings.

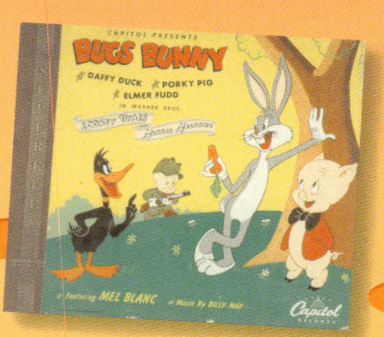

The specs don't help, Doc. Elmer's still fooled by rabbits in disguise.

The host with the least

Elmer parodied popular U.S. composer Deems Taylor as the host of the "Fantasia" segment of *A Corny Concerto*, a Merrie Melodies spoof of Disney's classical-music feature. His awe-inspiring gracelessness would seem hard to top—but nobody told Elmer, who later returned to host the TV parodies *This Is A Life?* and "The Sportsman's Hour" (in *Wideo Wabbit*).

As emcee, Elmer explains how the "wippling whythm of the woodwinds goes awound and awound and awound... and it comes out here!"

Man of distinction

"Elmer J. Fudd, Millionaire—I own a mansion and a yacht!" That's how our hunter identifies himself in *Hare Brush* under a doctor's hypnotic trance. Fudd has a full life outside of rabbit hunting, and our glimpses of it through the cartoons reveal a diverse range of interests. Pet lover (in *Hare Tonic*, above), screwball scientist (in *Hare Remover*, below left), farmer, vaudevillian, operatic viking, and T.V. show host are a few of the roles Fudd has excelled at in his long career of rabbit chasing.

Bugs has tricked scientist Fudd into drinking his potion which turns a normal character into "a devilish fiend!"

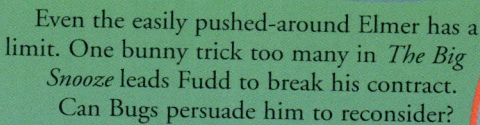

Even the easily pushed-around Elmer has a limit. One bunny trick too many in *The Big Snooze* leads Fudd to break his contract. Can Bugs persuade him to reconsider?

After pursuing Bugs into a vaudeville theater in *Stage Door Cartoon*, Fudd finds himself on stage doing embarrassing stunts and wearing ridiculous costumes.

Home from the hunt

Elmer's country house has seen many guests. He has unwillingly shared its living space with Bugs in *The Wabbit Who Came To Supper*, foolishly agreed to let Daffy be his slave in it in *Wise Quackers*, and defended it from a maniacal flea in *An Itch In Time*. In *Easter Yeggs* (below), Elmer decorated the house to try to lure stand-in Easter bunny Bugs to his doom. And when he came in—BOOM! Easter wabbit stew!

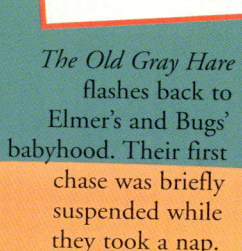

The Old Gray Hare flashes back to Elmer's and Bugs' babyhood. Their first chase was briefly suspended while they took a nap.

The Old Gray Hare also shows us Fudd in the future—a geriatric armed with a "Buck Wogers Wightning-Quick Wabbit-Killer."

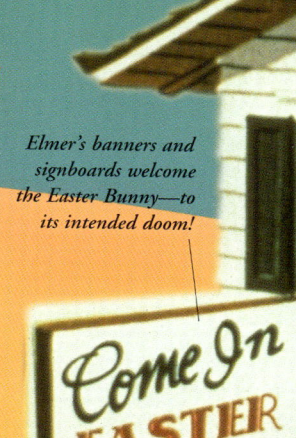

Elmer's banners and signboards welcome the Easter Bunny—to its intended doom!

TASMANIAN DEVIL

HE'S FAST AND FURIOUS and comes from a land way down-under. He's the all-devouring Tasmanian Devil—and he's Looney Tunes' wildest success story. Appearing in a mere handful of classic-era cartoons, the savage beast whirled and chewed his way to the top, unforgettable from his first moment on-screen. All of us love Taz—especially youngsters—perhaps because he's the party animal we might be if we dared.

By the book
In *Bedevilled Rabbit,* Bugs hitches a ride in an airlifted crate of carrots and ends up in Tasmania—right in the path of a stampede of terrified animals. Bugs, of course, stands firm, wanting to know what the commotion is all about. He stops a croc, who folds himself up into an alligator bag before flinging out a guidebook, with a helpful warning—cue the appearance of the local terror.

Taz likes vegetables, too. When he's on a run, he'll chew his way through trees, boulders, and shrubbery.

Spin cycle
Taz is that most unique of beings—a species with its own singular means of transportation. Circling dizzily through the woods at well over 78 RPM, the entire body of this whirling dervish is a weapon, eating or boring through anything with which he comes in contact.

Taz's only weakness is for music, as Daffy finds out in Ducking the Devil.

Taz doesn't always need a leg to stand on: When he goes for a spin, they're all off the ground.

38

Devil's food

The Tasmanian Devil will eat anything once, although he leans toward items that resemble animal prey. In *Devil May Hare*, Bugs is happy to oblige. Gum and bicarbonate of soda are combined to create a highly bubblicious chicken sculpture. Taz then gets to pig out on the "pig" (middle right): a disguised life raft that inflates inside the Devil. Talk about food filling you up fast!

Bugs exploits Taz's insatiable hunger by offering to cook for him—even when, moments before, the intended meal was rabbit!

Big boy

Taz has grown and changed from cartoon to cartoon. In Robert McKimson's classic monster model sheet (left) he appears as a walking stomach with a distinct underbite. More recently, the varmint has slimmed down and let his upper jaw protrude. But one thing has never been very clear: Taz's overall size. Sometimes he was much shorter than Bugs Bunny, while at other times he stood at precise hare height.

Devil with a purple bow

Unlike most other Looney Tunes, Taz is a married monster. Tasmanian She-Devil debuted and tied the knot in *Devil May Hare*, then struck back with a vengeance—and a rolling pin—in *Bedevilled Rabbit*, when she got jealous of a cross-dressed Bugs.

"All the world loves a lover, but in this case I'll make an exception." (Bugs, in Devil May Hare*).*

Not quite Mr. Manners, Taz spits out what Taz doesn't like. Pttooey!

High-tech Taz

The Tasmanian Devil's modern-day fame has led to a groundswell of merchandise tie-ins. Recent years have seen Taz starring with Bugs in video games and acting as NASA's Technology Applications and Space (TAS) project mascot.

YOSEMITE SAM

GREAT HORNY TOADS! Yosemite Sam may be small, but he sure is noisy! Sam first blazed onto the scene as a Western bandit, then evolved into an all-purpose villain who could pop up in any time, place, or guise. Hothead Sam may boast of being "the roughest, toughest, he-man stuffest hombre as ever crossed the Rio Grande," yet for all his macho bluster, he can never beat his arch-enemy, that "flea-bitten varmint" Bugs Bunny!

Sam's ten-gallon hat is nearly as tall as the bandit under it!

The more he yells, the more his mustache flaps!

A bandit is born
Director Freleng introduced Sam in *Hare Trigger*, a Bugs Bunny Western spoof. Writer Michael Maltese took the blowhard sheriff from *Stage Door Cartoon* and added a roaring voice inspired by Red Skelton's popular radio comedy character Sheriff Dead-Eye. Legend has it that Sam was also based on the famously fiery-tempered Freleng himself!

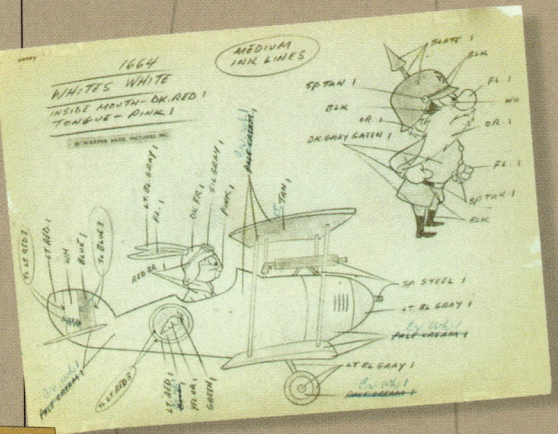

Mel Blanc claimed that Sam was the toughest voice to perform. "Imagine screaming at the top of your lungs for an hour and a half."

Dumb patrol
Sam's final Looney Tunes appearance was playing Baron Sam Von Shamm, a World War I flying ace, in *Dumb Patrol*—shown here in a color model sheet, which instructs the painters on the proper coloring for the animation. Heroic Bugs blasts Sam out of the sky and his ghostly image floats up toward heaven. Says Bugs, "I've heard of Hell's Angels, but I never thought I'd see one!"

Sam's name first appeared on a "Wanted" poster in *Hare Trigger*. Other names considered were Texas Tiny, Wyoming Willie, and Denver Dan.

In *Honey's Money*, Sam tries to get rid of his stepson Wentworth by encouraging him to play ball in traffic. But it's Sam who gets flattened!

Sam's sensitive side
Sam can be romantic—but he always has ulterior motives. He woos wealthy heiress Granny in *Hare Trimmed*, but ends up almost marrying Bugs Bunny (in drag). In *Honey's Money*, Sam weds a homely widow for her fortune, but gets landed with the task of entertaining Wentworth, her big slow-witted son.

Bugs Bunny's Granny disguise fools Sam in Hare Trimmed.

Sam-of-all-trades
Sam's personality is too big to be confined to the Old West. Wherever in the world there is gold to grab, money to scam, or rabbits to suppress, Sam will be there. He has appeared as Sultan Sam in Egypt, and Riff-Raff Sam in the Sahara desert; he's been a prison guard, a crooked politician, a claim jumper, and a castaway.

Sam's camel-riding skills are on a par with his horsemanship—pathetic!

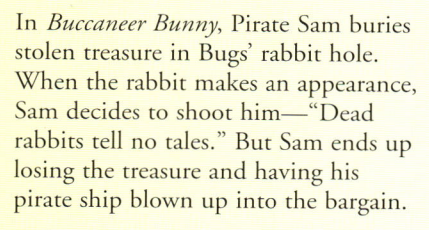

Soldier Sam
Whatever historical period Sam turns up in, he always has rabbit trouble! As a Viking called Sam the Terrible, he takes on Bugs in *Prince Violent*; he is Black Knight Sam in the Oscar winning *Knighty Knight Bugs*; Captain of the Guard in *Roman Legion Hare*; Sam Von Shamm, a German mercenary, during the Revolutionary War in *Bunker Hill Bunny*, and fiery Colonel Sam (above) in *Southern Fried Rabbit*.

In *Buccaneer Bunny*, Pirate Sam buries stolen treasure in Bugs' rabbit hole. When the rabbit makes an appearance, Sam decides to shoot him—"Dead rabbits tell no tales." But Sam ends up losing the treasure and having his pirate ship blown up into the bargain.

Sam has appeared in some unusual guises. In *Devil's Feud Cake*, he makes a deal with the Devil. In *Lighter Than Hare*, "Yosemite Sam from Outer Space" tries to capture Earth creature Bugs.

Pirate Sam
Sam is the only character to be well-known in two separate guises: as a Western bandit and a pirate. Pirate Sam only appeared in three cartoons, but they were memorable roles. Whether burying treasure, attacking tall ships, or putting down a mutiny, Sam was always pitted against a rabbit—and he always lost out to the "barnacle-bitten land lubber."

Sam plays "Shanghai Sam" in Mutiny on the Bunny.

41

PEPE LE PEW

BRASH AND OVERCONFIDENT. Hopelessly in love. Clueless about his body odor. Chuck Jones' Pepe Le Pew possesses a macho mindset that many men possess—but rarely practice. Jones described Pepe as "so sure of his appeal to women that it never occurs to him that his attentions might be unwelcome, or even offensive." It seems quite fitting that a character so full of love has become one of Warner Bros.' most beloved stars!

Le lover
Pepe was introduced in *Odor-able Kitty*, directed by Chuck Jones. In that film, a tomcat looking for food disguises himself as a skunk—only to attract the amorous attentions of a certain French Casanova. But this early version of Pepe is revealed in the end to be Henry, a henpecked American suburban-skunk.

Family man?
Family life is not for Pepe. After his debut film, which showed him shackled to a wife and kids, Jones revived the lovelorn skunk in *Scent-Imental Over You* as a swingin' single. This time he is named "Stinky" (on studio model sheets and on his mailbox in this film). In a location identified as Manhattan, he chases a Mexican hairless dog who is disguised as a skunk.

"YOU ARE SUCH A TEASE!"

"Permit me to introduce myself. I am Pepe Le Pew, your lover!"

Pepe is sure to mistake the red face of a cat holding her breath for blushing!

Animation drawing

Formula for success
Pepe's third film, *For Scent-Imental Reasons*, established the formula for the series: a female black cat would inadvertently get a white stripe painted down her back and become Pepe's "object of desire." When this cartoon won an Oscar, Pepe became a cartoon star.

A fresh stripe of white paint

Le pursuit

"It is love at first sight, eez eet not?" Pepe has pursued love in a wide variety of locales: The French Alps (*A Scent Of The Matterhorn*), a Foreign Legion outpost (*Little Beau Pepe*), a zoo (*Scentimental Romeo*), a movie studio (*Past Perfumance*), a cruise ship (*Who Scent You?*), and France's most famous art museum (*Louvre Come Back To Me*).

Sultan of love

Pepe's name and distinctive voice recall Charles Boyer, who played Pepe Le Moko, the romantic lead in the classic 1938 movie *Algiers*. Boyer's performance defined him as one of the screen's great continental lovers. *Cat's Bah* (shown here) pays homage, with Le Pew quoting Boyer's famous lines—"Come with me to the casbah." "Pepe's voice was warm and seductive," said voice artist Mel Blanc. "I was delighted because Gallic accents had been among the first I perfected as a child."

Background painting from Cat's Bah

Fifi

Pepe's first female conquest was a Mexican hairless canine called Fifi, in the film *Scent-Imental Over You*—originally titled "Forever Ambushed."

Pepe has many adult fans, perhaps because of his obsession with love. Very few Pepe toys were aimed at children!

Limited-edition statue (odor-free!)

The scent of Le Pew

"Pepe cannot know that he smells," wrote Chuck Jones. "He is clearly shocked to be informed about his odor in *For Scent-Imental Reasons*." In fact, Pepe is so shocked that he pulls out a gun and threatens to shoot himself ("I missed, fortunately for you").

La femme skunk fatale!

Pepe's reluctant main squeeze is the black cat officially dubbed Penelope but sometimes called Mam'selle Kitty or Fabrette. She is fast, clever at hiding, and an expert at holding her nose. "You know, it's not just a case of physical attraction," says Pepe. "I admire her mind, too!" Her greatest performance, however, was not with Pepe, but co-starring with Bugs Bunny in *Carrotblanca*!

Set in old New Orleans and narrated by June Foray, *Really Scent* tells of Pepe's only successful romance with "Fabrette"—yes, this is the cartoon where he gets the girl!

Pepe appeared in 17 classic films—including a cameo appearance in a Tweety and Sylvester cartoon, *Dog Pounded*.

43

MARVIN THE MARTIAN

WITH HIS TENNIS SHOES, scrub-brush headpiece, and timid, geeky voice, Marvin the Martian is an unlikely space tyrant. But the petulant alien considers himself far superior to Earthlings and thinks nothing of kidnapping rabbits or aiming very nasty Illudium PU-36 Explosive Space Modulators at irritating planets. Yet when he faces Bugs Bunny and Daffy Duck, it's always Marvin that ends up seeing stars!

K-9 and Bugs have their first close encounter in Hare Devil Hare.

Oh, I'm going to blow it up!

"You have made me very angry. Very angry indeed." Marvin may be small and controlled, but he's dangerous. When he peers through his telescope and discovers that Earth blocks his view of Venus, he calmly plans to destroy the irritating planet. "I patterned Marvin after the god Mars," said director Chuck Jones. "That was the uniform Mars wore—that helmet and that skirt. We thought putting it on this antlike creature might be funny."

Lieutenant K-9
Marvin's canine subordinate K-9 is truly a Martian's best friend. He willingly retrieves Earth creatures (often Bugs Bunny), but usually winds up in a straitjacket or unwittingly brings back lit dynamite sticks. "Delays, delays!"

Out of this world
Layout designer Maurice Noble did his most flamboyant work on the Marvin the Martian cartoons. Freed from earthly reality, he painted green skys, alien landscapes, weird spaceships, and pseudo-scientific apparatus, giving Marvin's universe the strong visual appeal of retro sci-fi. "He enhanced every story," said Chuck Jones. "If he got tired of all those cinematically overdone planets, he simply designed a city of delicately hued transparent plates floating in space."

Planet X
The barren Planet X is the universe's only remaining source of aludium fozdex, the prized shaving cream atom. Duck Dodgers and Marvin the Martian do battle to claim it. But this piece of prime intergalactic real estate is only big enough for *one* of them….

Marvin reaches the controls using his high-tech, height-compensating book stack!

K-9 signals danger by pointing at it.

MARTIAN MATOMIC MASHER

Martians in 3-D

Despite appearing in a just a handful of cartoons, Marvin's fame continues today. These maquettes were made for *Marvin the Martian in the 3rd Dimension*, produced for the Warner Bros. Movie World theme park in Australia. A combination of traditional hand-drawn cel animation and computer graphics, it is made to be viewed with 3-D glasses and is interactive—the audience is (lightly) assailed with steam and water!

Computer animators use maquettes to model the characters.

Bugs "evaporates" Marvin in *Mad As A Mars Hare*. In revenge, Marvin tries to send Bugs to a future of slavery with his Space-Time gun. But he accidentally sets it in reverse, turning Bugs into a prehistoric monster bunny.

Instant Martians

These strange, birdlike aliens first appeared as Jupiterians in the Porky and Sylvester cartoon *Jumpin' Jupiter*, but they became Instant Martians in the Bugs versus Marvin epic *Hare-Way To The Stars*. The wabbit accidentally transports a whole gross of them to Earth, as "gumball" sized seeds. They land in a sewer and spring to life.

Marvin was originally named Commander Flying Saucer X-2.

Marvin's trusty weapon—his Acme Distingerating Pistol

"I claim this planet in the name of Mars!" declares Marvin to Duck Dodgers.

Classic encounter

Marvin's best-known appearance was opposite Daffy Duck in *Duck Dodgers in the 24½th Century*. The cartoon was made during the height of a TV "space cadet" craze that saw heroes like Flash Gordon, Tom Corbett, Captain Video, and Buck Rogers save the universe on a regular basis. It inspired a sequel and a popular Cartoon Network TV series. The film director George Lucas was such a fan of the short, he arranged for it to play in selected theaters during the original release of *Star Wars*.

"DELAYS, DELAYS!"

On Mars, kilts are worn like tutu skirts.

Instant Martians grow from seeds when water is added.

Marvin's intergalactic spaceship, the Martian Maggot, with its sleek lines and angular stylings, was inspired by the UFO sightings common after World War II and the classic science fiction of the period.

FOGHORN LEGHORN

NOTHING, AH SAY NOTHING, gets past Foghorn Leghorn. He's matched wits with Daffy Duck, Pete Puma, and Sylvester. He's confronted beatnik roosters, hillbilly buzzards, and mischievous young chickens. And although he may get bruised, battered, and blown up, Foggy is the master of his barnyard domain. Stealing the show with his exaggerated movements and blustery blather, he's a true Southern star!

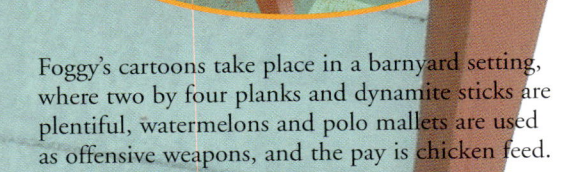

Foggy's cartoons take place in a barnyard setting, where two by four planks and dynamite sticks are plentiful, watermelons and polo mallets are used as offensive weapons, and the pay is chicken feed.

Loud mouth—Foghorn has a tendency to sound like a... well, a foghorn!

Large, overbearing body

King of the coop
Robert McKimson's loud-mouthed rooster made his debut as a supporting character in the Henery Hawk cartoon, *Walky Talky Hawky*. After a few cartoons, it became obvious that Foggy got all the laughs, so he was promoted to star. Mel Blanc based his vocal performance on a popular character played by actor Kenny Delmar on the Fred Allen radio show—the pompous Southern windbag, Senator Claghorn.

Foggy model sheet
A model sheet shows Foghorn, Barnyard Dawg, and a shades-wearing rooster. Although he is named "Banty," he is not the pinfeatherweight boxing champ Kid Banty who appeared in *Sock A Doodle Doo*. In fact, he is a beatnik rooster who pretends to be an orphan on Foggy's doorstep just to get in to see the "chicks."

Barnyard Dawg

The most frustrated character in Foggy's barnyard is the dog, known to Foggy only as "Dawg." He would love to knock out that windbag Leghorn—if only he could get loose. Yet as long as a certain "loud-mouthed Schnook" is free range, the Barnyard Dawg doesn't have a chance. As he says: "Some days it don't pay to get outa bed!"

"DOO DAH, DOO DAH!"

At times, Barnyard Dawg has been allied with Henery Hawk, Daffy Duck, Miss Prissy, Kid Banty (a prizefighting rooster), and the Weasel. But it usually winds up the same way: the dog gets whacked on his rear end.

All-too-short leash

"The little ol' lint pickin' weasel" was a frequent menace to the farmyard. But Foggy would always find a way to use him to bedazzle the dog.

Tough guy

"Nice kid, but a little dumb." That's Foghorn's opinion of the hungry chicken hawk who isn't quite sure who is or isn't a chicken. Chuck Jones created Henery but McKimson directed the little tough guy in *Walky Talky Hawky*, the Leghorn's debut cartoon, which was nominated for an Oscar.

Brainy bird

With his tiny body, big head, and large glasses, Egghead Jr. provokes in Foggy a fatherly desire to make a real kid out of him. But armed only with his brain, a reference book, and a slide rule, the little bookworm out-plays, out-kids, and outwits the rooster at every turn.

The love of Miss Prissy

Miss Prissy may be the one animal that Foghorn fears the most. His lifelong membership of Bachelors Anonymous doesn't stop the persistent spinster from trying to woo him—or the Barnyard Dawg from trying to fix them up. Prissy first appeared in the Porky Pig cartoon *An Egg Scramble*, trying to protect her one and only egg. Shunned by the snobby chickens in her roost, Prissy frequently gets the last laugh on them—and Foggy—with her trademark, "Yeeeeeeees!"

The look of love that sends shivers down Foghorn's spine

SPEEDY GONZALES

HE'S A HERO, a Romeo, and, above all, the catalyst for some very funny chases. Speedy Gonzales, "the fastest mouse in all Mexico," proudly upholds the honor of Mexican mice against foreign and domestic cats. Always ready to use his quick wits (and even quicker feet) to help his amigos, popular Speedy is also a big hit with "everybody's seester." This winning combination of a cheerful, upbeat nature and a fast turn of foot makes Speedy unstoppable, and ensures that he always gets the cheese!

A winning team
Speedy teamed up with "El Gringo Poosycat" (Sylvester) in the Academy Award-winning *Speedy Gonzales*, directed by Friz Freleng. It was to be a long (and fast-) running partnership.

South of the border
Warner's animators loved the Mexican motif and used it in a number of other cartoons. In *Tortilla Flaps*, the bullying Señor Vulturo tries to raid the mice's Mexican fiesta. Jose and Manuel (below) are two Mexicali crows who raid Elmer Fudd's cornfield in *Crow's Feat*.

Fast track to stardom
In Robert McKimson's *Cat-Tails for Two*, Speedy eludes two cats on board a Mexico-bound ship. *Speedy Gonzales* established the set-up of Speedy helping his hungry fellow mice by stealing cheese from a factory, store, or ship, usually guarded by Sylvester. Speedy regularly made life miserable for Daffy Duck, and has also appeared with Granny, Witch Hazel, Road Runner, and Wile E. Coyote in his many cartoons.

International star
Speedy's cartoons are popular not only in the U.S. and Mexico, but in Europe and around the world, as this Italian poster shows.

Mexican piggy bank mouse

The Spanish-speaking mouse has appeared in comic books, and as dolls and toys.

Scenic settings
Part of the charm of Speedy's cartoons lies in the stylized art of Mexican rural locales. This layout drawing of a village square, by Hawley Pratt (right), featured in *Gonzales Tamales*.

Speedy's slow pal
Speedy's cousin, Slowpoke Rodriguez, makes up for his lack of pace in *Mexicali Schmoes* and *Mexican Boarders* with his gunfighting and hypnotism skills.

"ARRIBA! ARRIBA!"

Catch him if you can, Pussy-gatos!

Mexican cats
Speedy is a legend throughout Mexico. But fame has a price—he is often pursued by cats who want the glory of catching the famous rodent. In the Oscar-nominated *Mexicali Shmoes*, directed by Friz Freleng, fat Jose and skinny Manuel try (and fail) to make a meal of Speedy.

In *Tabasco Road*, Speedy speedily substitutes a stick of dynamite in a cat's mouth for his friend Pablo!

DAZZLING DAMES

THE LOONEY TUNES appear to be a mostly male menagerie, but don't be fooled. They've got distaff star power too, and the Warner Bros. girls are one striking, saucy, and seriously screwball sorority. Young and old, sweet and sour, from dreamers to schemers to eating machines—all the female charmers are right here.

The Barnyard Dawg doubles as the Fudds' "Wover."

The world's worst wabbit hunter has at weast been wucky in womance. Elmer Fudd's equally dim, equally language-warping significant other helped her hubby face off with Daffy in *Don't Axe Me*.

Granny plays as hard as the rest!

Lola Bunny—Baseball pro... and a babe to boot

Spin sister
She might wear lipstick, a bow, and high heels but She-Devil is no fragile fashion victim. After Bugs marries her to Taz on-screen in *Devil May Hare*, the down-under wonder girl proceeds to snarl and spin as hungrily as her beau. She swings a mean rolling pin, too—effective in *Bedevilled Rabbit* when cross-dressed Bugs intrudes on her territory.

Chat room
Minding her own business in France, Penelope the Cat always manages to get a white stripe painted down her back. That's when skunk lover Pepe Le Pew arrives on the scene, pursuing the feline in hope of a stinky soiree.

Double dribble
The Tune Squad prove basketball amateurs in *Space Jam* until Lola Bunny arrives to show off a few moves... and curves. With her Bugs-enticing catch phrase "Don't call me doll!", Lola moved on from the feature film to become a recurring pizza delivery girl in the comics.

Mini-meow
Tiny Pussyfoot can melt the hardest heart, reducing bulldog Marc Antony to big-brotherly mush in Chuck Jones' classics *Feed the Kitty* and *Cat Feud*.

Daphne Duck

This she-duck's marriage to our despicable drake might have been a knot better left untied. For three cartoons—*Wise Quacks*, *The Henpecked Duck*, and *Quackodile Tears*—Daffy is a duck-pecked husband, kicked and slapped around by his demanding spouse. In the latter film, Daffy kick-starts a gator of a goof-up for Daphne when their egg rolls into a crocodile nest.

In *His Bitter Half*, Daffy has the proverbial wife three times his size.

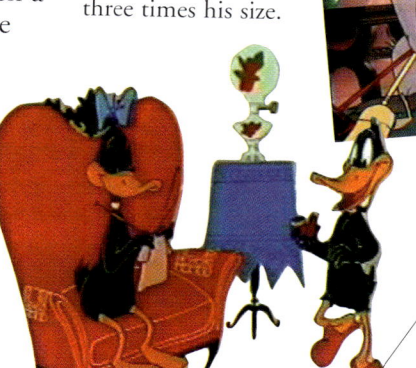

Slippers—the one sure sign of a married mallard.

Bugs' beaus

Romeo loves Juliet. Lois loves Superman. Porky loves Petunia. But Lola is only the latest in a long string of flings for our favorite—and not exactly committed—single rabbit. Perhaps finding a steady girl simply isn't a top priority for the wild hare with a closet full of skirts.

"Your teeth are like pearls—real ones, no dime-store phonies!", quoteth Bugs Bunny to Daisy Lou in *Hare Splitter*.

In *Hold the Lions, Please*, Bugs mocks a dopey king of the beasts for letting his girl "wear the pants in his family." Mrs. Bugs Bunny then appears to show us that she wears the pants in Bugs' family—literally.

Ye-es!

Geeky but determined Miss Prissy longs to snap Foghorn Leghorn into that ol' ball an' chain. The wistful widow hen is also proud mother to Egghead Jr., superbrainy offspring from an earlier flock.

Lady pig

The longest-lived Looney lady is Petunia Pig, introduced by director Frank Tashlin in *Porky's Romance*. Alternately sticky-sweet and terribly temperamental, Petunia starred in a mere handful of shorts. She went on, however, to feature in hundreds of classic comics, most notably Wild Western adventures with her rancher Uncle Ham. Petunia is also (confusingly) a cousin to Porky's nephew Cicero.

He's the apple of her sty!

Right in the kisser

In *Hare Splitter*, Bugs vies with rival rabbit Casbah for Daisy Lou's affections. When Daisy goes shopping, Bugs costumes himself as her and continues the romance in her absence, treating Casbah to some seriously unladylike billing, cooing, and clobbering.

Comic-book cutie

The comic-book saga *Showdown at Carrot Gulch* introduced Honey Bunny, a character created for print and merchandise. Honey was a starstruck fan who became Bugs' belle and constant companion.

GAG REFLEX

WELCOME TO THE AWARDS for the best-ever sight gags in Looney Tunes. Before we begin, let's remind ourselves of the cartoon laws of physics. Law #1: Cartoon characters do not study law. Law #2: See Law #1. This is why, when cartoon characters run off cliffs, they fall only when they realize that they are suspended in midair. (And even then, they might have time to wave bye-bye.) Now, let's celebrate the dazzling inventiveness of Looney visual jokes. Drum roll, please....

5 Portable hole

Some of the Warner Bros. directors had a rule of thumb for sight gags: for it to qualify as a cartoon gag, it had to be something that couldn't happen in live action. Road Runner demonstrates this important point with the classic moveable hole gag, seen here in *Beep Prepared*. Whether you put your finger in it and slide it across the ground, or as Road Runner demonstrates, pick it up and place it where you want it, the portable hole creates an instant hole and instant hilarity.

4 False tunnel

Trompe l'oeil is a French phrase that means "trick of the eye," or in the Coyote's case, trick of the whole body. Here, he paints a realistic-looking tunnel on the side of the mountain. This gag demonstrates Law #1 in reverse. Since the Road Runner doesn't know that it's a painting, he runs into the painted scene and off into the distance. But the Coyote, even having just seen the Road Runner defy physics, *knows* it's a painting and smashes right into it. Sometimes, it pays to be ignorant.

The Coyote is just too smart for his own good in this scene from Fast and Furry-ous.

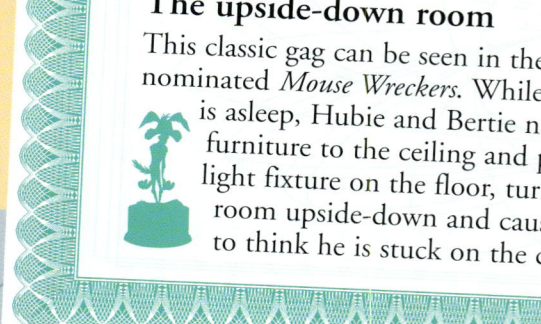

3 The unwitting dupe

Here's Daffy Platypus... er, Daffy Begonia... um, well, what's left of Daffy Duck, anyway. In *Duck Amuck*, Daffy runs afoul of the artist drawing him. From changing backgrounds in midstream to disappearing voices, it's one insult after another. Finally, Daffy puts his foot down and angrily berates the artist. Unbeknownst to Daffy, he is given this new floral look. It isn't kept a secret long, however, as the artist then draws a mirror for Daffy to see himself. This recurring gag can also be seen in the Bugs Bunny cartoon, *Hare Remover*.

Notice the flag on Daffy's tail that spells out "screwball."

JUDGE'S HONORABLE MENTION

The upside-down room

This classic gag can be seen in the Oscar-nominated *Mouse Wreckers*. While Claude Cat is asleep, Hubie and Bertie nail all the furniture to the ceiling and place the light fixture on the floor, turning the room upside-down and causing Claude to think he is stuck on the ceiling.

52

Supergenius?

It's only fitting that Wile E. Coyote wins the award for the funniest visual humor. After all, when you rarely speak, you have no choice but to rely on sight gags. Wile E. bristles at the notion that any of his brilliance was meant as gags, however. He blames the Acme Corp. for shoddy products, but refuses to switch because of their frequent-buyer program.

Coyote (Gloatius Maximus)

Coyote's award (Hunkiti Junkiti)

2 Avery's gags

Tex Avery was a king of the sight gag. His cartoon *Cinderella Meets Fella*, which stars the little bald funny guy Egghead as Prince Chow Mein, is full of them. When searching for Cinderella, Egghead finds her house courtesy of the subtle array of neon signs around it (left). Neon signs also point out otherwise-hidden locations in *Hair-Raising Hare*, where the front of the castle proclaims "Evil Scientist"; the gag is amended in *Water, Water Every Hare* with a flashing "Boo" sign. But perhaps the most inspired visual gag in *Cinderella Meets Fella* is the moment when Egghead tips his hat at the audience, but manages to tip his head as well (right)!

With startling visual gags like this, it's perhaps surprising that Egghead doesn't lose his head!

1 The inexplicable

As we have seen, the laws of physics do not apply to cartoon characters, especially if they know no better. Here, in first place, is a prime example. The Coyote holds up a solid steel plate to stop the Road Runner, but the Road Runner doesn't know he can't run through steel. So, he just goes ahead and does it, leaving a perfectly shaped outline of his body! But where is the Coyote's torso? This brings us to the inexplicable, meaning it can't be explained. What's more, if it could be explained, it would ruin the gag. You wouldn't want us to ruin the gag now, would you? We thought not.

Cartoon characters have often been known to go through walls, doors, windows, and the ground, leaving behind a silhouette of their bodies.

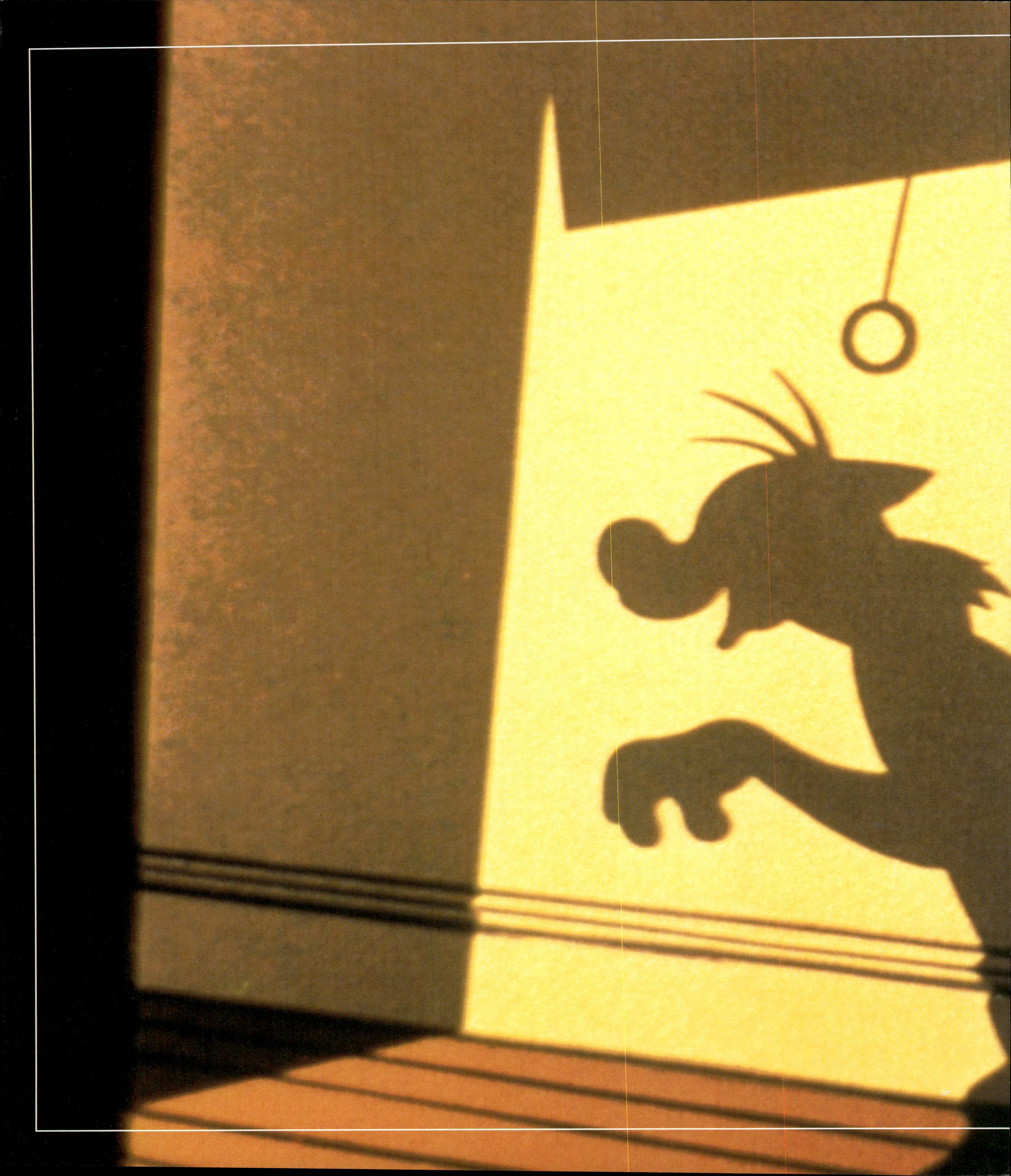

THE BEST OF ENEMIES

CAT CHASES CANARY. Coyote pursues bird. Sheepdog hounds wolf. These cartoon double-acts can't live with each other—but can't live without each other either. Their on-screen encounters have caused more fireworks than the Fourth of July. We love to watch, root for, and laugh at the feuds of these familiar foes who never know when to give up. They are truly "the best of enemies"!

CANARY

ALLEY CATS, BEWARE! Even without Sylvester, Tweety "taw" a variety of "puddy tats" and hilariously put them down with his lethal combination of innocence and brutality. In these films, Tweety is sweetly subversive and devilishly clever, with an arsenal of grenades, pistols, anvils, mallets, and dynamite sticks. "I get rid of more puddy tats dat way!" he chirps.

This tooth belongs to the not-so-clever cat in Birdy And The Beast.

Tweety appears on an animators' character sheet.

Catstello is the dumb one!

Little cherub

In Bob Clampett's *Wacky Blackout*, the tiny canary wants to be a dive bomber. The cherubic bird becomes a foil for a pair of felines in *A Tale Of Two Kitties*. The two cats, named "Babbit and Catstello," were intended to be the stars, but the little bird stole the show with his first words, "I tawt I taw a puddy tat."

A Tale Of Two Kitties

When Tweety appeared in a cartoon with tomcats Babbit and Catstello, the little bird dominated the comedy. The cats were reinvented as mice in later films directed by Frank Tashlin and Robert McKimson, and they chased after a less threatening goal—cheese.

Tweety walks the red carpet in Birdy And The Beast. Unfortunately the trail leads directly into a cat's mouth! Luckily, Tweety has brought along some matches to light the way....

From baby to birdy

Tweety appeared to be a tiny, defenseless creature beset by hungry predators, but he always managed to show up how dumb the hungry tomcats really were. Director Bob Clampett said of Tweety, "In school I remember seeing nature films which showed newborn birds in a nest. They always looked funny to me. This stuck in my mind: the helpless bird in a nest."

Despite his innocent air, Tweety knows how to confuse a cat. In these storyboard sketches for *Birdy and the Beast* (below), drawn by animator Rod Scribner, he substitutes his own body for a grenade!

PUDDY TAT

"**T**HUFFERIN' THUCCOTASH!" This lisped exclamation became the catchphrase of a perpetually hungry alley cat with a mania for chasing little birdies. With his big red nose, shthloppy grin, and legs like baggy pants, Sylvester resembles a circus clown. And even when he isn't teamed with Tweety, his clownish antics are hilarious when he plays such roles as a back-alley garbage cat or the leader of a gang of cat hoodlums!

Bulbous, clownlike nose

Sylvester plays the unlikely leader of a cat gang in Kitty Kornered.

Sylvester's voice
Mel Blanc provided Sylvester's unmistakable voice. "A big sloppy cat should have a big, shthloppy voice," he recalled. The cat's voice is actually identical to Daffy Duck's—the only difference being that Daffy's is speeded up after it is recorded.

Porky's pet
The "bad ol' puddy tat" co-starred in a variety of films without Tweety. Bob Clampett's *Kitty Kornered* featured Sylvester as Porky Pig's pet cat. He becomes leader of a group of lazy housecats determined to remain indoors on a cold night. The crew don Martian costumes to drive Porky crazy—and hopefully out into the snow.

Kitty Kornered featured Sylvester with some fellow felines. However, the cat mostly hunted Tweety, Speedy, or Hippety Hopper alone or with his son.

After throwing Porky out of his own house, Sylvester's gang in Kitty Kornered *party on, caterwauling "Auld Lang Syne."*

Woodpecker trouble
In *Peck Up Your Troubles*, Sylvester is set against a wily little woodpecker who evades every attempt at capture. When Sylvester hangs on a branch, the woodpecker greases it so the cat slips, then pecks a dotted line and cuts along it. Finally, the bird tricks the tomcat into thinking he's squashed it, causing an attack of guilt!

Layout artist Hawley Pratt drew this sketch of the woodpecker.

SYLVESTER AND TWEETY

SYLVESTER HAS HUNTED other prey and Tweety has outwitted other cats. But when they get together, this pair has a special chemistry that has won them two Oscars and millions of fans. And although Sylvester has been roughed up countless times by the innocent-looking canary, he just can't stop trying—he's a cat possessed. For this "bad ol' puddy tat," canary is always the first choice on the menu.

"I DID SEE A PUTTY TAT!"

Trick or tweet
Sylvester has tried numerous tricks to catch Tweety. His disguises include dressing up as a bellboy, a wildlife photographer, a scarecrow, a chicken, a lamp, and a tree. He has also pretended to be Granny and Batman, built robot dogs and rockets, and mastered flight by strapping an electric fan to his back—all to no avail.

On an electric fan-powered flight to Tweety's cage in Tweetie Pie.

Cat meets canary
Tweety and Sylvester first crossed swords in the cartoon *Tweetie Pie*. In this film, Tweety is taken in by the cat's owner. Despite being warned to leave the bird alone, Sylvester tries to get his paws on Tweety, leaving himself (and the house) in a shambles. Freleng's pairing of the two characters was a brainwave, resulting in a hit that gave Warner Bros. its first Academy Award for a cartoon.

Warren Foster's original storyboard panels from Red Riding Hoodwinked

Behind bars
The main function of Tweety's birdcage is to keep Sylvester out rather than to keep Tweety in! The canary spends most of his time swinging, singing, or eating bird seed behind bars, while Sylvester cooks up his latest scheme. The cage is not impenetrable, however: In *Tweetie Pie* (top left), Sylvester tries to enjoy canary-under-glass, but the bird negotiates a release—poking the cat's paw with a sharp pin.

An original background painting from Greedy For Tweety *shows Tweety's little sick bed. In this film, Tweety, Sylvester, and Spike are each laid up with a broken leg.*

Story writers
Warren Foster was Friz Freleng's chief storyman during the prime of Tweety and Sylvester. His strength was writing stories with clear structures. "The other guys could come up with wild gags," recalled Freleng, "but you really had to connect them to make a decent story."

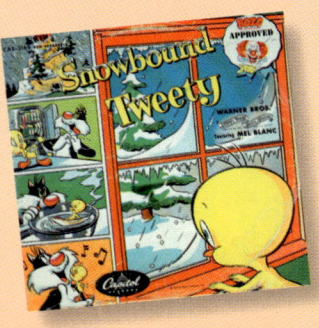

Though the cartoons were popular with adults, Capitol Records produced a line of Tweety phonograph recordings aimed at kids. This one is loosely based on the cartoon *Snow Business*.

Purr-fect puss

Sylvester has many fine qualities that make him the ideal house cat. He has incredible patience (particularly when waiting for Granny to leave the house so he can chase Tweety again). He's also housebroken (in other words, he's broken everything in the house!).

Sylvester wants his owner to think he is an angel—so she'll leave him alone with Tweety!

Sylvester has a lot on his mind: breakfast, lunch, and dinner!

Sylvester only has two plans for Tweety—to catch him and to eat him (and, yes, Tweety is a boy).

Bulldog Spike

Spike the bulldog (a.k.a. Butch, Hector, or, as Tweety says, "puddy dog") often stands between Sylvester and his canary sandwich. The cat confronts a giant-sized Spike in *Tweety And The Beanstalk*—and a whole yard full of "Spikes" protect Tweety from cat attacks in *Ain't She Tweet*. Sylvester could not escape the canine even in non-Tweety capers—and in *Pappy's Puppy*, Sylvester is harrassed by Spike's tenacious son.

In Gift Wrapped, Granny knows how to have a peaceful Christmas!

Dog pound

In *Dog Pounded*, Tweety takes refuge in a tree in the middle of a dog pound, leaving Sylvester to find a way past the canines. Hypnotism, a swing, and a rocket fail, but a skunk's white stripe painted down his back finally gets the dogs on the run. The cat discovers an unwanted side effect, however, when he finds himself in the embrace of amorous Pepe Le Pew!

Where Sylvester wants Tweety

Tweety as Robert Louis Stevenson's infamous horror character Mr. Hyde

A rare sight—Tweety in Sylvester's clutches!

This maquette was sculpted for the film Space Jam.

Leaves footprints all over Granny's house.

In *Hyde And Tweet*, Sylvester dreams that Tweety drinks Dr. Jeckyll's formula and becomes a giant "Mr. Hyde" monster. The cat samples the formula himself in *Dr. Jerkyl's Hide*, when he aims to terrorize bully dogs Spike and Chester.

59

THUFFERIN' THUCCOTASH!

WHEN HE IS NOT chasing Tweety, Sylvester has a separate career co-starring with Speedy Gonzales, Hippety Hopper, and a slew of miscellaneous mice. He annoys the likes of Elmer Fudd, Foghorn Leghorn, and Porky Pig, and falls victim to bully dogs Spike and Chester. Considering how often he gets zapped, bashed, and clobbered, the tomcat needs more lives than the average cartoon cat. In his career at Warner Bros., Sylvester has certainly inspired nine lives of laughs.

Acme Batman outfit

In *Satan's Waitin'*, Sylvester uses up all nine of his cat lives chasing Tweety. He is shipped off to a Cat Hades ruled by a satanic bulldog. Of course, he was revived in time for his next cartoon.

Big loser

Sylvester can't seem to catch a break—or anything else! In *Mouse Mazurka*, he chases a polka-dancing rodent loaded with nitro glycerine. In *A Kiddie's Kitty*, a destructive little girl "adopts" Sylvester, loads him into the washing machine and blasts him into space. *A Mouse Divided* sees him becomes the "father of a breakfast" due to an inebriated stork delivering a baby mouse to Mr. and Mrs. Sylvester J. Pussycat. Then there's tough city dogs, Spike and Chester, who beat him up in two Friz Freleng-directed cartoons, *Tree For Two* and *Dr. Jerkyl's Hide*.

Sylvester encounters Spike and his hero-worshipping colleague Chester in Dr. Jerkyl's Hide.

When clobbered, Sylvester sees little Tweety birds.

Sylvester and Porky

Chuck Jones occasionally recast Sylvester as Porky Pig's cat. As a pet, Sylvester could not speak and was therefore unable to warn his accident-prone master of danger.

Sylvester's on his back again.

Sylvester has had his tail pulled off on numerous occasions!

Best supporting player

Sylvester was one of the most reliable character actors in the Warner Bros. cartoon stock company. Sometimes, the animators would also cast the cat in juicy supporting roles. As the villainous Grand Duke in *The Scarlet Pumpernickel*, he has a swashbuckling fencing duel with Daffy Duck.

Sylvester about to get in more trouble!

"I WANT A MOUSE OF MY VERY OWN, TO LOVE HIM AND PET HIM...."

Dumb cat

In *Hoppy Go Lucky*, Sylvester goes hunting for a meal with a big, dumb cat named Benny (voiced by Stan Freberg). This character parodies Lennie, the dim-witted hulk featured in John Steinbeck's 1937 novel *Of Mice and Men*. The "mouse" in this cartoon is Hippety Hopper and the "man" is Sylvester, whom Benny dubs "George"—when corrected, Benny replies "But I can't say Sylvester, George!" The boneheaded Benny has better luck in his next film, *Cat Tails For Two*, where he goes after Speedy Gonzales.

Bag for catching normal sized mouse.

Elmer and the kitties

Sylvester finds another sparring partner in Elmer Fudd. In *Kit For Kat* (above), Sylvester competes with a cute kitten for Fudd's affections. As a result of his efforts, Fudd is evicted and ends up competing with Sylvester for a trash-can feast. Their feud hits a high note in *Back Alley Oproar*. As a singing alley cat, Sylvester makes Fudd fume with a midnight concert that includes Hungarian Rhapsodies and Spike Jones-styled pop tunes.

The fastest mouse in all Mexico.

Gringo pussycat

Friz Freleng relocated Sylvester south of the border in his Oscar-winning cartoon *Speedy Gonzales*. As guardian of the cheese, the "gringo pussycat" was drowned in tabasco sauce and dragged through the desert—all in pursuit of the rapid rodent and his Mexican muchachos.

Sylvester competes with Sam, a gooney orange cat colleague, for dinner—first for Tweety in *Trick Or Tweet*, then for a mouse meal in *Mouse And Garden*.

Sam voiced by Daws Butler

Cat and rooster

Sylvester met his match when Robert McKimson placed him in the farmland domain of Foghorn Leghorn. In *Crowing Pains*, Foggy convinces Henery Hawk that Sylvester is a chicken. To prove it, he arranges for Henery to hear Sylvester crow at dawn—and he does! The lesson from this: A putty tat should beware of a rooster studying ventriloquism!

GOOD RELATIONS

SYLVESTER ONLY has Tweety on his mind, except when she has to worry about the canary's protective owner, Granny, or his own demanding son, Sylvester Jr. Not to mention a boxing kangaroo named Hippety Hopper! They complicate his life, exasperate his best-laid plans, and—worst of all—witness his most humiliating failures.

Granny always wears her hair in a tight bun.

Bea Benaderet first voiced Granny, after which June Foray took over.

Granny
Tweety and Sylvester's owner, kindly old Granny, has zero tolerance for the cat's schemes. She has been known to hide in Tweety's cage in order to smack Sylvester with her umbrella or dress up as T.V. character Ralph Kramden to sock him—"Pow! Right in the kisser!"

In Tweety's S.O.S., *Sylvester alters Granny's glasses for "Tweety vision." To Granny, it looks as if the canary is safe in his cage—in reality, the cat is chasing the bird around an ocean liner!*

Pampered pets
Granny dotes on her pets—Tweety, Sylvester, and a bulldog called Spike. In *Greedy For Tweety*, she nurses the bedridden trio who, despite their broken bones and heavy casts, continue to chase, clobber, and blow each other up, leaving Granny to sigh, "que sera sera."

A model sheet, designed for Friz Freleng's unit, shows the old lady in various moods and positions for the animators' reference.

Without Tweety
Granny has made a few solo appearances. In *Corn On The Cop*, policemen Daffy Duck and Porky Pig chase the octogenarian, whom they suspect is a disguised thief, around town. Yosemite Sam woos Granny for her money in *Hare Trimmed* (below), but the old lady is saved from his clutches when Bugs dresses up as her and gives Sam a nasty shock at the altar.

Pop 'Im Pop! was the third appearance of the "giant mouse" and the first film to feature Sylvester Jr.

A model sheet shows Hippety as he first appeared.

Hippety Hopper

Sylvester may boast about hunting "king-size mice," but one particular king-size mouse keeps our cat confounded. Hippety Hopper is really a baby kangaroo who first escapes from the zoo in *Hop Look And Listen*. The mute marsupial confuses Sylvester in over a dozen more films, punching and pouching the pussycat, who never once questions the existence of a four-foot rodent—he only knows he must catch it, and he's unable to admit defeat. "Why, I wish he was twice as big..." brags Sylvester at the end of *Pop 'Im Pop!*, in which Hippety appears in the pouch of his twice-as-big mama—Gracie, the Fighting Kangaroo—a sight which has Sylvester running back to a canary diet.

Hippety as he appeared in later cartoons by Robert McKimson.

Junior always looks up to his pop.

Sylvester Jr.

This lisping littl'un is desperate to believe his father's tales of mouse-catching glory, but regularly has his bubble burst by Sylvester's humiliating failures. Director Robert McKimson and writer Warren Foster introduced Junior in *Pop 'Im Pop!*, the first of a series of father-son cartoons which leave Sylvester's self esteem in tatters, and Junior hiding his face in shame.

Background painting

In *Birds Of A Father*, Sylvester shows his son a high-tech method for catching birds—like the one Junior has become friends with. "Oh father, are we cannibals?" he asks, to which Sylvester laughs back, "Yeah-heh-heh-heh!"

Final scene with cel overlay

Parental guidance

Sylvester is always eager to fulfill his fatherly duties. He takes his son cat-fishing in an aquarium in *Fish And Slips*—and gets trapped in a "dog-fish" tank! In *Goldimouse And The Three Cats*, his efforts to defend his home from a rodent end with his family fleeing to a backyard bomb shelter.

In *Cat's Paw*, the junior scout risks losing face when Pop takes him bird stalking—and is beaten by a baby eagle.

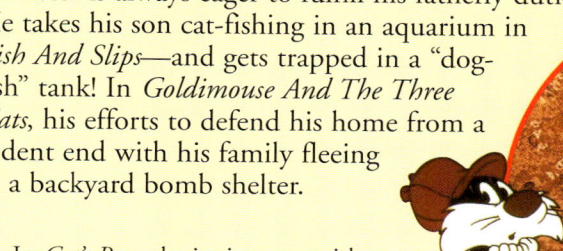

Tail usually between his legs.

ACCELLERATII INCREDIBUS

(Otherwise known as Velocitus Delectibus, Super Sonicus, and Speedipus Rex.)

ROAD RUNNER & WILE E. COYOTE

"BEEP-BEEP!"

This Road Runner toy bank could help the Coyote save for a new Acme device.

ARMED ONLY with a fork, a knife, and a catalog of clever contraptions, a pathetic desert scavenger chases an impossible dream. This simple premise has been keeping audiences laughing for years—and the Acme Corp. in the black. Beep-beep! Zip-dang!

There they go-go-go!

Director Chuck Jones and writer Michael Maltese decided that each Road Runner cartoon would consist of 11 blackout gags that would build to a strong finish. So no matter how many bat-winged flight suits, rocket powered roller skates, and large coil springs the coyote uses, it's been preordained that this duo will keep chasing into the sunset.

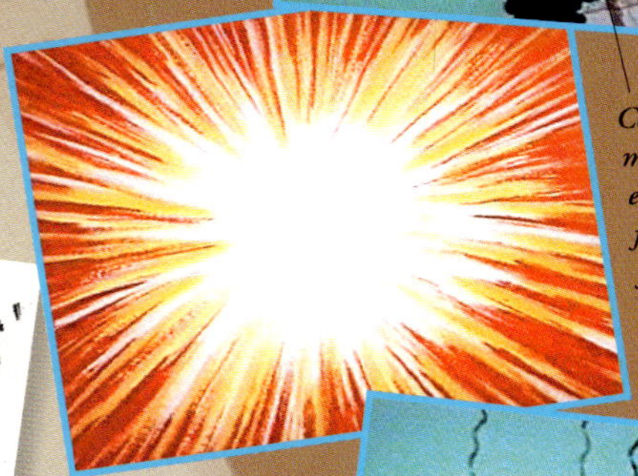

Coyotes were never meant to fly—especially not with five gallons of rocket fuel strapped to their back!

In *Fast And Furry-ous*, the Coyote tries out his first Acme product—a "Super" suit. (It doesn't work.)

Road Runner

The Coyote actually caught the Road Runner once, in *Soup Or Sonic*. But the coyote was reduced in size and had to grab onto the bird's giant-sized leg. He holds up a sign to the audience that said, "Okay wise guys, you always wanted me to catch him. Now what do I do?"

Beep Beep and Kelsey

The original comic book version of the Road Runner and Coyote differed from its animated cartoon source. Most notably, the Road Runner spoke in rhyme, called himself "Beep Beep," and had three young Road Runner nephews.

The coyote makes his first appearance in a story with Henery Hawk, who identifies him as "Kelsey" Coyote!

Taking the fall

Gravity is the Coyote's greatest enemy. In *Whoa Be Gone*, the famished canine gets the bright idea to put a trampoline on the spot in the canyon where he keeps landing. Unfortunately, instead of stopping his fall, the Coyote crashes through it.

There really is a bird called the Road Runner, but it doesn't cry "beep-beep!" or run at 100 miles per hour. Early sketches of the Coyote and Road Runner show that a more realistic character design was considered.

Treading air

"The only enemy the Coyote has is his overwhelming stubbornness," said Chuck Jones. "Like all of us, at least some of the time, he persists in a course of action long after he has forgotten his original reasons for embarking on it."

The dream of a Road Runner dinner.

Wile E. Coyote

"The Coyote is a history of my own frustration and war with all tools, multiplied only slightly," said Chuck Jones. The director had a set of rules for the character which included: "No outside force can harm the Coyote—only his own ineptitude or the failure of Acme products."; and "The Coyote could stop anytime—if he were not a fanatic!"

As Chuck Jones stated, "The Coyote is always more humiliated than harmed by his failures."

CARNIVOROUS VULGARIS

(Otherwise known as Hardheadipus Oedipus, Eatibus Almost Anythingus, Caninus Nervous Rex.)

DESERT HUNT

THE AMERICAN DESERT is the coyote's natural location and Wile E.'s operational base of choice. Everything about it makes sense. It's the traditional home of Road Runners and rabbits. It's filled with natural hazards that a crafty predator can use against his prey. And its flat roads make for easy delivery of Acme's hazard-causing products.

Balancing rocks don't stay balanced for long.

Acme wrecking ball: may unpredictably wreck your best-laid plans

Wile E. Coyote makes a strong impression.

Giant rubber band: throws coyotes at passing trucks

Burmese tiger trap: surprisibus, surprisibus

Acme catapult armed with coyote-seeking rock

Cut rope, release anvil, feel the pain.

Grenade flume: built in two weeks, destroyed in five seconds

TNT: the Wile E. weapon of choice!

The pause that refreshes: Wile E. Coyote waits to fire until just the right moment—and invariably gets it wrong.

Usual spot where Wile E. realizes he's no longer on land

Field of operations

A sophisticated hunter works with every element of the landscape. In this desert terrain, ledges make handy spying points and excellent launch sites for missiles, while crevasses provide ready-made pitfalls, and basins are perfect spots from which to fire rockets upward. The only trouble with the desert is that its advantages can become disadvantages when your prey is unwilling to accept that you are a supergenius.

Hazards

If a truck hits a coyote in the desert and nobody notices, has he really been clobbered? The answer is yes—motor vehicles forever ambush Wile E. at the most uncomfortable times, and with the most deceptively Road Runner-like sounds. Beep-beep!

The common locomotive is big trouble for the Coyote. They don't just hit him—they carry him miles away from the Road Runner.

The one spot where the Road Runner is totally safe!

Acme cannon: ready, aim, backfire.

Dead-end bridge: for chasing your prey over the edge.

Acme grease: to send you down the slippery slope

High bridge: good for looking down on lesser creatures

Wile E. mines his own business.

Painted truck tunnel: beware of beep-beeping!

Birdseed: tempting, aromatic, boobytrapped

Unlit mine shaft: strike match, find TNT stockade.

Bugs' desert home: Albuquerque, New Mexico

Three-wheel rocket: when two wheels just aren't enough

The painted desert

Parts of this prairie don't really exist—or do they? Artist as well as predator, Wile E. makes landscape paintings to disguise Road Runner-trapping cliffs and dead ends. But the images turn frustratingly real—and artificial once again—usually whenever it's least convenient for the Coyote.

ACME CORP.

WELCOME TO Acme's latest catalog! Here you'll find the finest in quality hardware, high-tech gadgetry, vitamin supplements, unique fashions... and birdseed. Our products are shipped to you immediately for instant use. Just call the toll-free number or send the mail-order form today. You'll be glad you did. And remember, if we don't make it—you don't need it!

Boom-erang
Guaranteed to return at speed, this little weapon from Down Under has won rave reviews from boxing kangaroos and Tasmanian Devils.

Warning: Do not throw near to boulders, electricity wires, supplies of dynamite, or at Road Runners!

Tornado Kit
Nothing makes a stronger statement than your own personal tornado. Amuse your friends and fix your enemies! Forget "Spin the Bottle," the grow-your-own tornado kit is the perfect party game. It will leave you dizzy for more! (Trailer parks not included.)

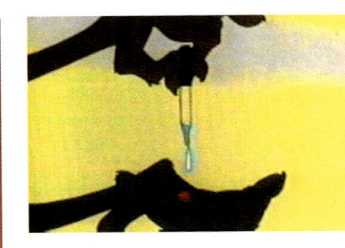

Dehydrated Boulders
Dehydrated for easy shipping and storage, these boulders are filled with artificial rocklike material. Just add water, stand back, and watch them gain weight and swell to enormous size. We guarantee nobody will want to be crushed by one of these babies!

Regular buyer Mr. W. E. Coyote of Southwestern Desert ready to take off.

Jet Motor
Multi-use: attach handlebars and ride, strap to back and fly, or tie to feet and jet-ski! Watch out for realistically painted tunnels on rock walls. Comes with handheld sign: "How about ending this cartoon before I hit?"

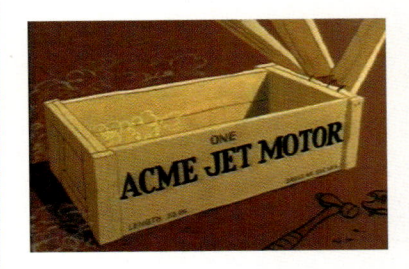

HEN GRENADE
Keep your sunny-side up with these exploding pre-omelets. All hungry coyotes will find them the ideal offensive weapon against offensive fowl—*eggs-actly*! Powerful enough to blow the feathers off 20 birds. Crack open a crate of Hen Grenades today!

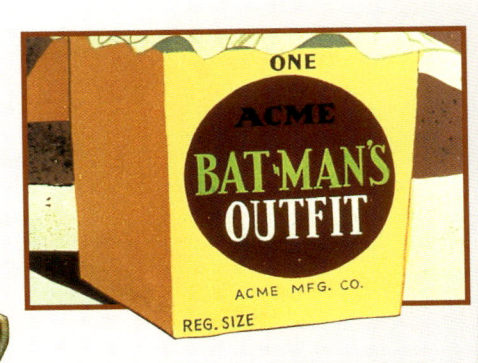

Bat-Man's Outfit
This skintight, green-leather jumpsuit may be worn in desert conditions and is long-lasting, comfortable, and just a little bit naughty, with or without underarm bat-wing attachments. *Warning: If you attempt to fly in this costume, look where you're going! Legal notice: This costume is in no way connected with Batman the comic-book character.*

Regular customer Mr. Coyote demonstrates the versatility of our Bat-Man's outfit.

Bird Seed
Road Runners just won't be able to resist this delicious, low-fat birdfood. Acme Bird Seed is also suitable for Henery Hawk, Daffy Duck, Foghorn Leghorn, and Tweety. Every Granny should keep a six-month supply.

Warning: Do not mix with ACME Iron Pellets. "Free lunch!" sign not included.

SPECIAL OFFER!

Rocket Skates

Calling all hunters: Why go to all the trouble of strapping a giant wind-sail propelled by an electric fan to your back? Our all-new, rocket-powered roller skates offer all the speed you will ever need and are just dandy for extreme sports, racing, hunting, and chasing. Also available as inline blades and as skateboards.

BEDSPRINGS

OK, we admit it. Beds don't use springs much any more, and we have to move these things somehow—but wow, *what a deal!* A special favorite with people too cheap to buy a pogostick. Put a spring in *your* step!

EARTHQUAKES

At last—the power of an earthquake in pill form. Experiencing a personal earthquake is every bit as enjoyable as being in a *real* one!

Small print: Ineffective on road runners—very effective on coyotes!

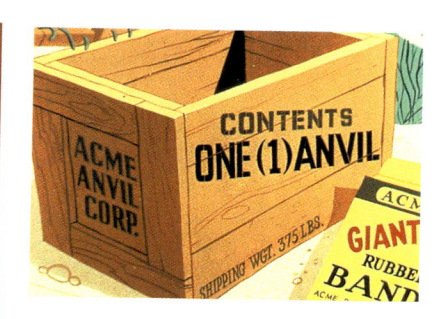

ANVIL

Our Number One product! Who would have thought it would be so popular? Nothing beats an anvil for hunting small desert animals and fowl. It's sleek, aerodynamic, and lasts and lasts and lasts. Once used by blacksmiths to hammer metal into shape—now more famous as a cartoon prop! It's heavy, dude!

POGO STICK

An Acme pogo stick takes you where you want to go in more time than it takes to walk—not to mention making you dizzy and disheveled. Our jet-propelled model does it even faster. Get the jump on your friends!

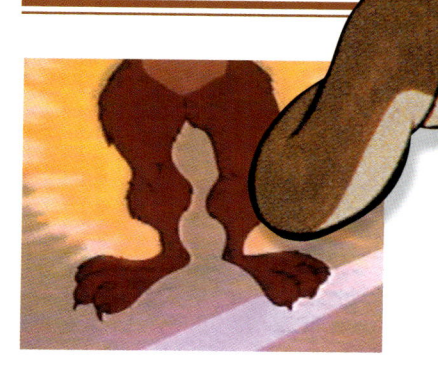

Vitamins

Bulk up your calves, pump up your shins, and run for your life with our Leg Muscle Vitamins! Eyelid, earlobe, and pinky vitamins also available!

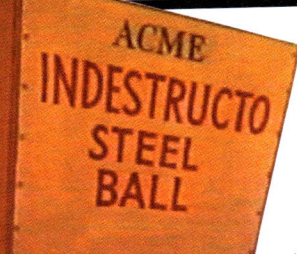

INDESTRUCTO STEEL BALL

A must for all those who enjoy a brisk roll down a sharp, two-mile decline over jagged terrain. This assault-vehicle has absolutely no moving parts to wear down, no unreliable, fancy extras such as a rearview mirror or a steering device, and no unnecessary frills such as brakes. The Indestructo Steel Ball is just 800 pounds of rampaging, steel-smashing fun! Climb aboard for the ride of your life!

High concept, low success rate

If complexity alone were a guarantee of victory, these intricate attacks would surely have gotten the Coyote his bird. However, the more pots you stir at once, the harder it is to get a Road Runner into one...

In *Fast and Furry-ous*, Wile E. created an instant snowdrift to ski to the Road Runner—with predictable results!

This plan, from *Beep, Beep*, would've worked... if only the wire had been tighter.
1. Carry anvil out onto tightwire
2. Drop anvil on Road Runner
3. Road-Runner burger

1. Freezer
2. Icemaker
3. Meat grinder
4. Easy-to-ski snow trail

Wile E.'s reading list includes cookbooks and Acme catalogs.

SUPERGENIUS

FOR WILE E. COYOTE, simply catching the Road Runner isn't enough—he wants to do it smartly. This self-proclaimed "Supergenius" puts an intellectual spin on each game plan or hardware combo he uses. But his brainpower soon gives way to egotistical fanaticism. As Chuck Jones said of Wile E., paraphrasing philosopher George Santayana: "A fanatic is one who redoubles his effort when he has forgotten his aim."

Card-carrying coyote: Wile E. first flashed his credentials in *Operation: Rabbit*.

Wile E. Coyote
Genius

Easy doesn't do it

Logic says that simple Road Runner capture schemes should succeed where the more complicated ones fail. Au contraire: Wile E.'s simpler efforts are just as failure-prone. Nevertheless, you have to admire that careful planning, that attention to detail, that creative coyote brain, that—SPLAT!

A plan from *Fast and Furry-ous* that looked foolproof on paper.

❶ Pull out key stone
❷ Rock falls
❸ Road Runner
❹ Road Runner crushed (ha-ha!)

Wile E. adopts his thinker's pose. It's not his first statuesque moment. In *Going, Going, Gosh!*, quick-drying cement did the trick.

It's a supergenius requirement that blueprints be admired before use.

Wile E.'s overconfidence in his brainpower is highlighted in his battles with Bugs. In *Compressed Hare*, a distinctive mailbox fails to impress the bunny...

...and the coyote's attempt to rope him in is equally unimpressive. Whatever Wile E. tries, the rabbit is always traveling one knot faster.

Almost there

Far from being discouraged by his near-misses, Wile E. Coyote feels they only serve to vindicate his genius. Some of his schemes really do bring him tantalizingly close to the Road Runner—only to have fate intervene in the shape of an unexpected boulder! Next time, perhaps, next time....

The drawing board

A supergenius never gives up! The coyote has never considered throwing in the towel, even though he invariably ends up battered. In his comic book guise, insurance salesman Daffy tries to convince Wile E. to take out a policy. Silly duck!

RALPH AND SAM

WOLF WANTS SHEEP. Sheepdog protects flock. Everyone's got a job to do, right? The premise behind a series of cartoons directed by Chuck Jones is that two clever adversaries are pitted against each other as a matter of daily routine. Sam Sheepdog and Ralph Wolf punch in the timeclock every day at nine, outfox each other all morning, then take an hour for lunch. They resume their jobs in the afternoon and punch out at five.

Identical twins?
Wile E. Coyote and Ralph Wolf: similar-looking characters in slightly different roles. They look alike, dream alike, and at times they even scheme alike. Outside of the wolf's red nose they could be considered identical twins—since they also share a father in director Chuck Jones.

First outing
Ralph and Sam first appeared in *Don't Give Up The Sheep*. The Wolf learns that it takes more to get past the guardian dog than setting the timeclock ahead, tunneling under the sheep, ordering an Acme Wild Cat, or even disguising as a sheepdog, the Greek god Pan, or a bush.

Quick draw
Model sheets show how much work goes into the simplest aspects of making an animated cartoon. The director, or his character designer, created hundreds of poses for the animators to use as reference. Their "model sheets" ensured the character would be drawn the same from scene to scene.

No matter what the scheme, Sam is always there. Unlike the Coyote in the Road Runner series, Ralph Wolf frequently catches his prey. His problems start when Sam appears—usually at every turn.

Going undercover
The Wolf has no end of clever disguises to trick the Sheepdog. Among other masquerades, he has dressed as a knight, Little Bo Peep, and a rock (using an Acme Artificial Rock Suit). The most elaborate disguise gag occurs in *A Sheep In The Deep*, where the wolf and sheepdog try to top each other in a duel of disguises. Both are shown unmasking from dozens of guises, including sheep, horses, and even each other. The standoff only ends when the five o'clock whistle bows.

Sam appears to have eyes in the back of his head.

Disguised as a rock, or burrowing below the sheep, Ralph is in for a big surprise.

The sheepdog union must be very strong. Sam knocks off strictly at five and Fred Sheepdog takes over for the night, usually beginning his shift by resuming the beating Ralph was getting. Ralph, however, enjoys excellent health benefits and sometimes rides home in an ambulance.

"MORNING, SAM" "MORNING, RALPH"

Ralph's ultimate goal.

Dog of routine
Though Sam's eyes are covered by his red hair, nothing escapes his view or interferes with his daily routine. He eats his lunch at noon, and punches out Ralph Wolf at regular intervals.

Sam's red-haired mop top doesn't distract him from his job.

Ralph Wolf
"Ralph Wolf was a storyman at Warner Bros. cartoons," recalled Chuck Jones, "and I gave his name to the red-nosed version of the Coyote." Jones also gave him the Coyote's unique brand of supergenius. "Ralph lives across the street from Sam," said Jones. "And in the morning they come out together chewing doughnuts, greet each other, walk to work, punch the clock, and take up their professional positions."

Sam Sheepdog
"The Sheepdog is always aware of Ralph's every move," said director Chuck Jones, "but I don't know how he sees through that curtain of hair. I could have drawn long hair only over his nose, but I felt that his hair should be long everywhere. Even his feet are hairy, and when he sits down, I put a little fringe of hair where his bottom meets the ground."

Sam made a rare cameo appearance in Carrotblanca.

Sam keeps his bone sandwiches in his lunchbox.

The time clock signals lunchtime and quitting time for Sam—and sometimes Ralph, if he isn't in the middle of being punished.

CAUTIONARY TALES

WHAT LOONEY TUNE is complete without a plan that backfires—usually spectacularly—on its perpetrator? These cautionary tales occur often in chase sequences: Cat chases mice, cat chases bird, bird chases worm, coyote chases bird, wolf chases sheep, pig chases sheep and... well, you get the idea. The main basis for a chase is a number of try/fail gags. The chaser tries to catch the chasee, often with an elaborate plan, and then fails. So let's hear it for the best-ever worst-laid plans. May we have a kaboom?

Sylvester, humble and proud—until he learns that this is actually a booby prize!

5 Free drink of water
In Chuck Jones' cartoon, *Beep, Beep*, the Coyote sets up a booby-trapped drink of water to lure his prey. As the Road Runner approaches, the Coyote hides behind a boulder. The Road Runner just passes by the glass of water and zips in beside the Coyote, holding up a sign that says, "Road Runners can't read and don't drink." Frustrated, the Coyote chases the Road Runner through several other gags. Finally, after being launched by rocket-powered roller skates, bruised and battered, the Coyote crawls over for a refreshing drink—only to be blown up by his own device!

Bad ol' puddy tat
Tweety helped decide to bestow Sylvester with the Award for Most Backfired Gags. That's because Tweety contributed to many of them as the object of Sylvester's desire. Not to mention the gags that he caused to backfire!

4 Boulder over
Here is a classic setup and backfire from the cartoon *Steal Wool*. Having procured one of those patented giant rubber bands, Ralph Wolf is stretching it back in anticipation of launching a rock at Sam Sheepdog in order to catapult him off the cliff. Instead, the boulders to which the rubber band is attached pull out of the ground and spring back, sending Ralph flying through a narrow pass in a cliff, where he grabs hold of a tree. The tree rips apart, and Ralph sails backwards, grasping the tree trunk. He winds up pinned against a cliff side, where the boulders and debris smash into him. Say, just where does one get those giant rubber bands, anyway?

A case study of a backfiring plan. Don't try this at home!

JUDGE'S HONORABLE MENTION

Straightjacket to Mars
When Marvin the Martian is commanded to bring back one (1) Earth creature, he picks on Bugs Bunny. After getting Bugs into a straightjacket, Marvin's canine lieutenant K-9 falls for the old "this jacket just ain't my size, have you got something a little more sporty?" routine... doh!

2 Slammin' Sam
If curiosity killed the cat, then impatience might have killed Yosemite Sam. In the cartoon *Ballot Box Bunny*, Bugs decides to run for mayor against Sam and issues the challenge, "Anything you can do, I can do, only better!" Sam asks him if he can play the "pi-anny," to which Bugs responds, "Ya got a pi-anny?" Sam runs off to fetch one and rigs an explosive charge to go off when a certain key is struck. Bugs attempts to play the song "Those Endearing Young Charms" (apparently a favorite song among one-finger piano players), but twice plays the wrong note, thus skipping the booby-trapped one. Frustrated, Sam runs in to show him how to play it and... backfire!

Mayoral candidate Sam attempts the impossible: to get a fellow cartoon character to correctly play "Those Endearing Young Charms" on the piano.

3 Operation: grab it!
One of the plans in *Operation: Rabbit* finds Wile E. Coyote building a cute explosive female bunny robot. He switches it on to lure Bugs out of his rabbit hole. But at that moment, there is a knock on the door. Wile E. finds an attractive female coyote on the other side and commences to woo her, not noticing the wires coming off her back and leading out the door. The other end of the wires are attached to a detonator in Bugs' rabbit hole. Of course, all that is required now is for Bugs to push the plunger. As a dazed Wile E. sings "Here Comes the Bride," the rabbit robot begins to ring. Wile E. rushes to toss it out the window. Too late! Boom!

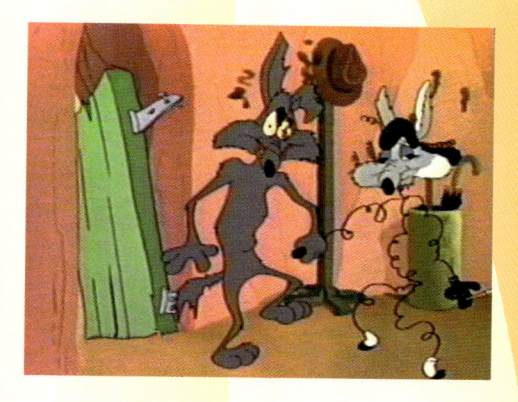

When Bugs fights fire with fire, Wile E. Coyote is the one fired upon.

The never-ending chase
Sylvester's whole life is an endless chase after the seemingly unobtainable Tweety bird. Yet what a chase! It has stretched across every location imaginable, from forest and cities to trains, zoos, circuses, snowbound cabins, and ocean liners—not to mention fictional settings such as Little Red Riding Hood's forest and Jack's beanstalk. And still the hapless Sylvester pursues his animal instincts with the most human of means—including saws, hammers, fishing rods, and desk fans.

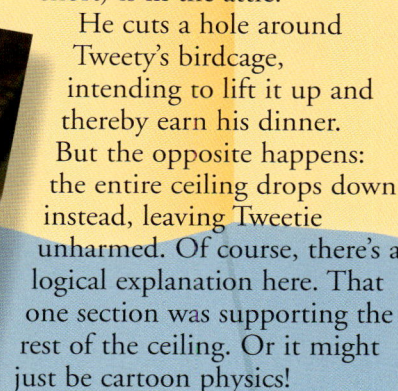

A surprised pussycat takes an impromptu backfire high dive.

1 I came, I sawed, I screwed up
A classic example of a backfiring plan lies in the frames of *Tweetie Pie*, directed by Isadore "Friz" Freleng. This gag is dependent on the idiosyncratic laws of cartoon physics—which are often liberally applied in an effort to invoke *Humorious Spasmodicum*, otherwise known as "laughter."

The plan seems simple. After many failed attempts, Sylvester (or Thomas, as he is called in this short) is in the attic. He cuts a hole around Tweety's birdcage, intending to lift it up and thereby earn his dinner. But the opposite happens: the entire ceiling drops down instead, leaving Tweetie unharmed. Of course, there's a logical explanation here. That one section was supporting the rest of the ceiling. Or it might just be cartoon physics!

75

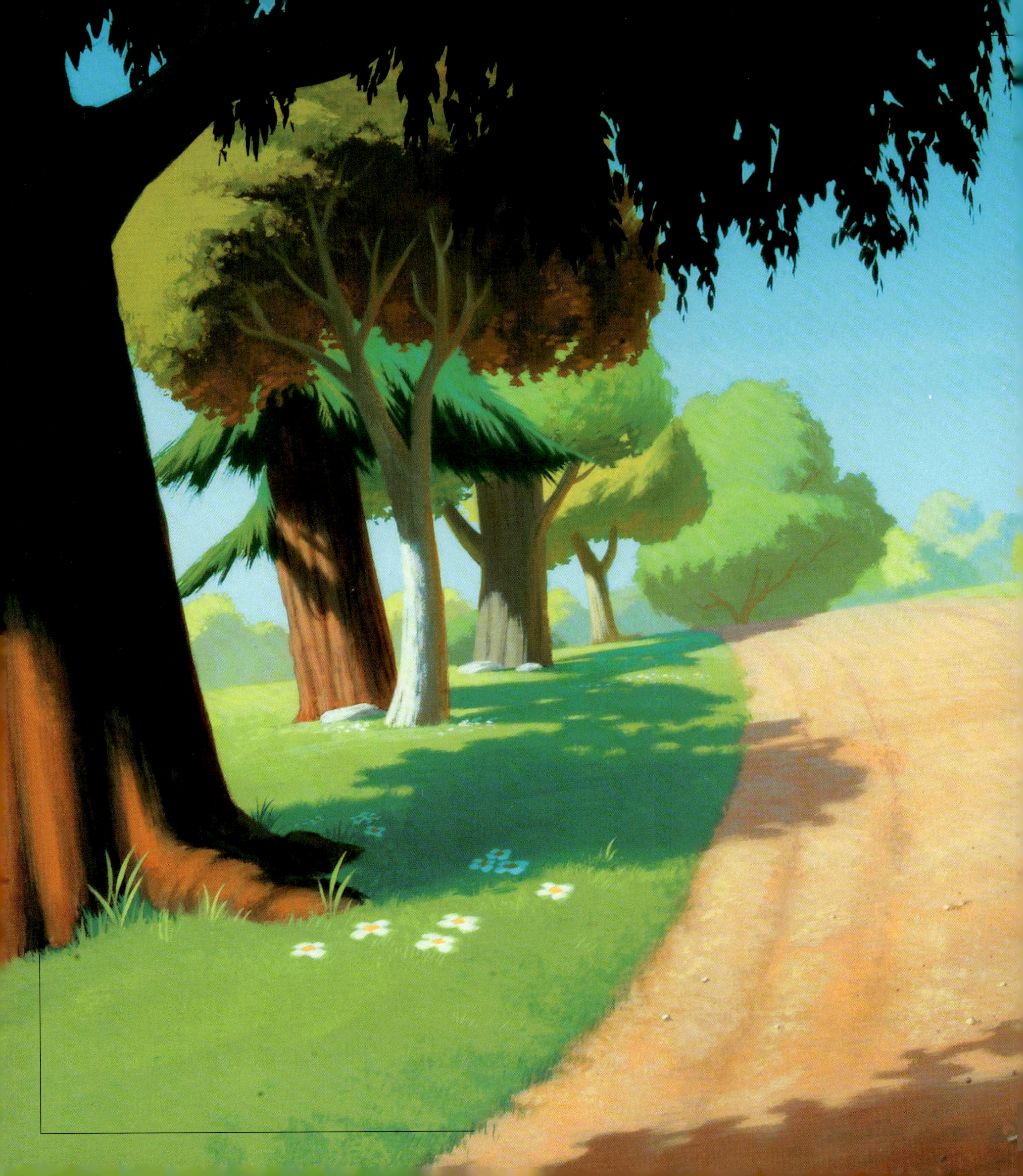

PUMAS AND GOPHERS AND BEARS, OH MY!

THE LOONEY TUNES animal kingdom isn't a monarchy—it's an anarchy! Pete Puma, Spike and Chester, Charlie Dog, and Cool Cat reign supreme, while humanized critters like The Three Bears and Cecil Tortoise act out fouled-up fairy tales. And let's not forget those rather more instinct-driven varmints, Henery Hawk and the Goofy Gophers, with their screwy insights into nature's way.

SNIFFLES

SNIFFLES THE MOUSE got his name because, in the cartoon *Naughty But Mice*, he had a cold and snuck into a drugstore looking for medicine. Sniffles was a Chuck Jones star who appeared in a dozen cartoons that had great appeal to children.

Little mouse

Sniffles was an innocent and childlike Warner Bros. star. His stories were always shown from a child's point of view. *Bedtime for Sniffles* shows the little mouse trying to stay awake on Christmas Eve long enough to see Santa Claus arrive. In *Toy Trouble*, Sniffles hides from a cat among the toys in a human store. The little mouse gets even with the feline and becomes a hero in *Sniffles Bells The Cat*.

Sniffles teamed up with a human girl named Mary Jane in *Looney Tunes and Merrie Melodies Comic*. Mary Jane had the power to shrink down to mouse size and had numerous magical adventures with her whiskered friend.

Sniffles' squeaky voice was provided by actress Bernice Hansen.

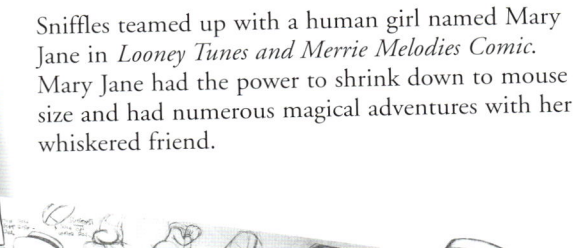

Chuck Jones' animation unit used this Sniffles the Mouse character sheet.

Sniffles' pork-pie hat is often mistaken for a sailor's cap.

Bookish best friend

Sniffles' best friend and companion is a silent bookworm whom he first meets when a bookshop comes to life in *Sniffles and The Bookworm*. In *The Egg Collector*, the two of them go on an exciting hunt together. After reading about how barn owls are harmless, feeding mainly on small rodents (and not realizing that he is a rodent himself), Sniffles and the Bookworn bravely pursue a baby owl egg under the watchful eye of a hungry Papa Owl.

"Do you really know where there's an owl's nest?" Sniffles asks the silent Bookworm in *The Egg Collector*.

Nice guys finish last!

In his final cartoons, Sniffles had a more vigorous personality as a cheerful chatterbox. Yet the little mouse was eventually outshone by newer stars who acted like adults and who could outwit adversaries rather than hiding from them.

The owl appears, the bookworm faints—will he and Sniffles escape?

CECIL TORTOISE

CECIL TORTOISE appeared in just a handful of cartoons, and each one was a winner. Cecil is notable as the only character who regularly managed to outwit Bugs Bunny, in hilarious and irreverent rewrites of Aesop's ancient fable *The Tortoise and the Hare*.

A model sheet shows some of Cecil's cousins from Tortoise Beats Hare.

Drawings from Rabbit Transit *illustrate the animation process.*

First challenge
In Tex Avery's *Tortoise Beats Hare* (below), Bugs walks on screen during the opening credits and is outraged by the title of the film. He calls for a race to prove the animators wrong, but Cecil beats the bunny with the aid of a few tricks and some strategically placed relatives along the race course.

Endgame
In Friz Freleng's *Rabbit Transit*, the tortoise uses a rocket engine in his shell. But Bugs uses his legs to win this final match. When the tortoise asks him how fast he was going, the bunny replies, "a hundred, easy"—so Cecil has him arrested for speeding!

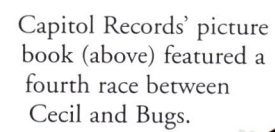

The rematch
Bugs challenges Cecil to a rematch in *Tortoise Wins By a Hare* (below right). The rabbit dons a streamlined tortoise shell in the belief that it will improve his aerodynamics. Unfortunately, the rabbit gambling ring bets everything on the hare to win, but Cecil, dressed as a bunny, is helped over the finish line, while Bugs as the tortoise is clobbered by his own brethren.

Capitol Records' picture book (above) featured a fourth race between Cecil and Bugs.

Cecil is the only star who could retire happily after defeating Bugs.

GOOFY GOPHERS

THEY'RE CIVILIZED, vegetarian, and oh-so-polite. The Goofy Gophers are the two most well-mannered pests ever to infest a garden. They may be brutally ruthless about getting their veggies, but they go about it in a hilariously genteel way that uniquely distinguishes them from their fellow Looney Tunes.

Spot the difference

Mac and Tosh, Tosh and Mac: who can tell them apart? From their appearance in *The Goofy Gophers* to the present day, the two farmyard raiders are visually indistinguishable—only their voices, provided by Mel Blanc and Stan Freberg, differ markedly. In the end, it hardly matters who's who: each gopher would graciously trade names with his partner if it made the other happier.

The Gophers share Bugs Bunny's preference for carrots.

The Gophers appear on this model sheet with chubby cheeks and their eyes alternately blase and naively startled—it's a polite appearance that cleverly conceals the characters' inner demons.

An original Gophers model sheet suggests more of the rascals' devilish side.

Polite to a fault

"After you," says Mac to Tosh. "No, after you," Tosh responds. You'd never guess the two were deciding who should go first to bash a dog with a shovel! Mac's and Tosh's hypergenteel manners reflect a humorous type of an earlier era—a fop so refined and cultivated that he seemed never to show real emotion. The comedy in mixing such figures with unrestrainedly wild slapstick seems obvious today—but the Gophers were there first.

Mac and Tosh usually live in underground chambers, which they dig themselves beneath gardens for quick access to a variety of vegetables. Now and then, however, they take up residence in a tree to partake of nuts, squirrel-style.

Mac gets ready to perform a scene from Hamlet *in* A Ham In A Role.

Acting up
In *A Ham In A Role*, a pompous dog actor tries to switch from comedy to Shakespearian acting. Mac and Tosh bring the high-and-mighty hound down to earth by enacting famous scenes from The Bard—with a twist!

Ghostly gopher
"Alas, poor Yorick, I knew him well...". When the Bard-obsessed pooch hams up Hamlet, the Goofy Gophers decide to put the shivers in his Shakespeare. Cowardice is the skeleton in doggie's closet—so "Yorick" Gopher's return from the grave is one scene Fido didn't need to see.

Joke book
A Ham In A Role discovers Mac and Tosh asleep in a hollowed-out copy of *Hamlet*. They've apparently been living there for a while, as no matter what Shakespearian stanza the dog may recite, the Gophers are ready with a preplanned embarrassing comeback.

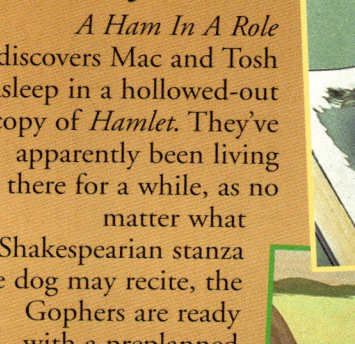

When the thespian hound asks to "drink the joy of life" (*á la Romeo and Juliet*), he gets a tub of water poured on his head!

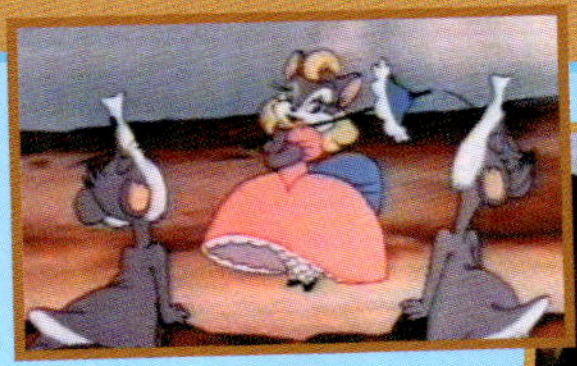

Gentlemanly Mac and Tosh whirl a girl over the garden dance floor in *The Goofy Gophers*, then find the she-gopher is really a hand puppet worked by a dog. The fake femme is sent off with a bang—TNT style.

Guard dog
The Gophers' classic foe is a lanky pooch who resides in a striped kennel (shown above in an original background painting). In *The Goofy Gophers*, the Gophers batter him with mousetraps, rocket launchers, boulders, and boxing gloves. When the dog thinks he's seen them off, he retires to his headquarters for a nap—but the gophers quietly strap him to a rocket and launch him toward the moon!

In classic cartoon tradition, the dog wears gloves over his paws!

81

"I LOVE MY PA"

THE THREE BEARS

ONCE UPON A TIME, there were three bears: a papa bear, a mama bear, and a baby bear. Sounds familiar, right? But here's where any similarity between Warners' triple bruins and a certain fairy tale ends. For while the original three bears led a happy life disrupted only by Goldilocks, Henry Bear, Ma, and Junyer are the definition of dysfunction—the bears most likely to live *un*happily ever after.

Junyer is the picture of brainpower—well, maybe not.

Ma hides her hidden depths well.

Bear essentials

In *Bugs Bunny And The Three Bears*, directed by Chuck Jones, the Three Bears initially set out to mimic their nursery namesakes. The grizzlies brew carrot soup and pretend to go for a walk, planning to lure a Goldilocks home for eating purposes. Too bad for the Bears, their "Goldilocks" turns out to be a wise-guy wabbit who plays the situation for a joke—assisted by the feuding family's own ineptitude.

Junyer gives his pop a friendly bear hug.

Bear roots

Henry, droopy Ma, and giant Junyer show their best and worst sides in an animators' model sheet. The Bears' look has changed little over the years—except that Henry's hair was originally black before becoming brown.

Junyer is generally twice Pa's size, but now and then he has been drawn even larger.

Baby Bear

Overgrown Junyer—voiced by Stan Freberg—is a bouncing seven-and-a-half years old, but he still wears diapers and sleeps in a cradle. Junyer's wits and coordination are similarly underdeveloped. The boy swats Henry with a shovel when aiming for a bee in *The Bee-Deviled Bruin*. In *A Bear For A Punishment*, he lovingly shaves Henry with a broken-down razor, not realizing it will leave Pa in stitches.

Henry Bear

"What have I done to deserve such a family?" Good question! While seeing himself as a long-suffering everybear, Henry actually has a near-psychotic bad temper. Ignoring Ma's good advice and bullying Junyer, "Pa"— voiced by Billy Bletcher—really has himself to blame for most of his unbearable bruises.

Cranial bandages make a hot head hotter.

Ma Bear

"But Henry...." Long-suffering Ma Bear—voiced by Bea Benaderet—is a deceptively simple figure. She unexpectedly reveals great dancing skill in *A Bear For Punishment*, all the while keeping the same stoic face. And in *Bugs Bunny And The Three Bears*, Ma reveals her sizzling romantic side—just in case you didn't think she had one.

Home sweet home

Classic Three Bears cartoons locate the fractious family in a cave kitted out like a house (right)—or is that a house kitted out like a cave? In their comic book appearances, the family has traded in its cliffside for a standard-issue woodland cottage (below).

It's what you do with what you've got—especially when you're a bear!

In *What's Brewin', Bruin?* the Bears try to hibernate, but all possible obstacles (especially Junyer) prevent Henry from sleeping.

In *Bear Feat*, Henry learns the folly of tightrope biking with a very heavy son.

Big-shows bruin

Great performers they're not, but Ma and Junyer do their best to entertain. In *Bear Feat* (above), the plan is to practice a moneymaking vaudeville act, hence the balancing and tossing of an outraged Henry. Then, in *A Bear For Punishment*, Junyer's and Ma's Father's Day pageant involves them in poetry recitations and military salutes.

Junyer's weight brings the tightrope to the ground.

The wire holds; Pa's temper snaps.

Agatha and Emily

Abracadabra! Meet Agatha and Emily, a lovesick, two-headed she-vulture who chases after sinister Count Bloodcount in *Transylvania 6-5000*. Unluckily for the Count, Bugs' magic words have turned him into a two-headed male vulture!

Delivered by stork via the "Pig & Duck, Nip & Tuck Delivery Service."

In a playful parody of Walt Disney's *Fantasia*, the Bob Clampett-directed *A Corny Concerto* features a villianous vulture who plays the harp on his way to heaven.

Bugs teases the none-too-bright Beaky Buzzard in *Bugs Bunny Gets The Boid*.

A pencil animation drawing.

Owl Jolson

Little Owl Jolson, the cherubic star of Tex Avery's *I Love To Singa*, is a wide-eyed crooner born into a family of classical music experts. Professor Fritz Owl, his papa, is horrified that his son wants to be a jazz singer—until he learns his boy is up for first prize on "Jack Bunny's" radio amateur hour!

Beaky Buzzard

In *Bugs Bunny Gets The Boid*, shy Beaky Buzzard is sent out by his Mama to get food. Instead, he gets a drubbing by Bugs Bunny. Beaky fails again to get dinner when set against a dinosaur named Shorty in *The Bashful Buzzard*, a lion in *The Lion's Busy*, and a papa sparrow in *Strife With Father*. In spite of his few on-screen appearances, Beaky was a mainstay of early Looney Tunes merchandising.

Odd birds

The surreal Dodo Bird from *Porky In Wackyland* (right) is the battiest bird in the menagerie. He can appear anywhere and stretch any body part. At the other end of the spectrum, the Minah Bird (below) in Chuck Jones' "Inki" cartoons is completely Zen. The silent, droopy-eyed bird walks into the scene, gives a little hop step, and compels the other characters to follow him wherever he goes—all accompanied by Mendelssohn's *Fingal's Cave Overture*.

In Looney Tunes, storks deliver babies to parents—usually the wrong ones. In *Stork Naked*, a blotto bird tries to deliver an egg to Mr. and Mrs. Daffy Duck and, in *Apes of Wrath*, a sloshed stork brings Bugs Bunny to Mr. and Mrs. Gruesome Gorilla. Storks also bring Bugs a bundle of little bunnies from heaven in *A Feather In His Hare* (above).

BIRDS OF A FEATHER

THEY WALK, THEY TALK, they sing jazz! These wacky winged characters have left an indelible impression as stars, co-stars, foils, and foes. They're Looney birds with only one thing in common (besides their feathers): They're funny. Whether they seek chicken, corn, or singing lessons, and whether they hunt Bugs, Foghorn, or Speedy, this feathered flock succeeds with flying colors!

"I WANT A CHICKEN NOW!"

Fighting spirit
Henery has large plans for his future. That's why, in *The Foghorn Blows At Midnight*, he is inspired by the great chickenhawks in history, such as John Paul Chickenhawk (above). His desire for greatness causes the barnyard dog and Foggy to continually fight over him. Says Henery, "I don't care who wins. I'll fricasee the loser!"

Henery Hawk
The little chickenhawk with a big appetite made his first appearance in Chuck Jones' *The Squawkin' Hawk*, establishing his relentless resolve for a hot chicken dinner. After that, Henery was abandoned for a few years, until director Robert McKimson and writer Warren Foster put him in *Walky Talky Hawky*. This time, however, he was upstaged by a bigger personality: Foghorn Leghorn. Henery also appeared with Daffy Duck in Jones' *You Were Never Duckier*. Here, Daffy disguises himself as a rooster in an attempt to win a big-money prize at a poultry show—and ends up having to evade Henery and his papa.

Preliminary character sketches for Henery Hawk

Henery featured as a supporting player in many cartoons, but snared even larger audiences in comic books and records.

PETE PUMA

LOCK UP THE LITTLE ONES, here comes Pete Puma! On second thought, don't worry about locking anyone up. As Foghorn might say, "This boy's about as sharp as the flat end of a nail." Although Pete only appeared in one theatrical cartoon, directed by Robert McKimson, no one can forget this punch-drunk pussycat who'll always interrupt his hunting for tea with the enemy.

Funny feline

"A-heeeeeeee"—Pete's laugh, provided by Stan Freberg, is instantly recognizable. It sounds like a cross between comedian Frank Fontaine and nails scraping a blackboard. Pete thinks he's a formidable predator, when he is actually a pushover. Bugs is still a tiny bit cautious: "I don't trust that sneakin' puma no further than I can t'row da big moe!"

Pete has a sweet tooth—he can't resist an offer of sugar lumps.

Hands—is he praying? He should be!

Pete takes things into his own hands.

Rabbit's Kin

In *Rabbit's Kin*, a small rabbit enlists Bugs' help when being pursued by Pete Puma. Bugs sets out to teach Pete a lesson or three. Pete reappears in an unconvincing disguise claiming to be the little fellow's mother. Later, Bugs turns the tables when he disguises himself as Pete's cousin, Paul Puma.

Bugs in puma costume

How many lumps? Pete never seems to learn that Bugs' question is not a civilized offer of sugar for his tea. When Pete responds, "Give me three or four lumps," Bugs obliges by whacking him with a mallet, giving him three or four juicy lumps on the head. Eventually, poor Pete decides that tea gives him a headache.

Pete and Foghorn

Pete has also appeared with Foghorn Leghorn in a new theatrical short, *Pullet Surprise*, directed by Darrell Van Citters, and in the Looney Tunes comic books.

Pete sinks his teeth in.

GOSSAMER

"**M**ONSTERS ARE the most in-n-n-teresting people," says Bugs of the seven-foot-tall bundle of joy known to his close friends and associates as Gossamer. With bright orange hair, a raspy, growly voice, and sneakers, Gossamer is so terrifying even his reflection runs away from him!

Spooked!
Bugs meets the monster in *Hair-Raising Hare*, directed by Chuck Jones. He follows a mechanical female rabbit into a castle where he is to be the monster's dinner. Bugs makes his exit: "And don't think it hasn't been a little slice of heaven... 'cause it hasn't!"

In a quick-change routine, Bugs becomes Gossamer's manicurist. The monster is in for a painful surprise as he dips his "little patties" in the water—where two primed mousetraps await him.

Claws for alarm! Seriously, these hands need a manicure.

An interesting monster should have an interesting hairdo.

"PEOPLE... GRRRRRR!"

More monstrous fun
In *Water, Water Every Hare*, Bugs again confronts the monster with no visible nose or neck. This time he plays hairdresser, blowing up the monster with dynamite rollers before shrinking him to the size of a mouse.

Canned Monster! Look for it wherever creepy products are sold!

COOL CAT & CO

NEVER CONTENT TO REST on their laurels, the Warner Bros. animators constantly tried out fresh ideas, offbeat stories, and wild new characters. The later rabbits, cats, mice, and Martians will never eclipse the fame of Bugs or Daffy, but they are always funny and original—and every bit as Looney as their predecessors.

Sports star
Cool Cat becomes top athlete at Disco Tech in *Bugged By A Bee*, when a bee's strategically timed stings spur him to spectacular feats in baseball, rowing, and pole vault.

A beret keeps this cat cool.

Cool Cat
Groovy Cool Cat is clearly in tune with the swinging times in which he was created. The "hep-talking tiger" eludes capture by Colonel Rimfire in his own laid-back style. Cool Cat ends one cartoon by saying to the audience, "So cool it now, ya hear?"—which could almost have become a catchphrase for this groovy Looney Tune.

A hard hat for a hard head

Cool Cat heats up as the captain of the rowboat team in Bugged By A Bee.

Colonel Rimfire
British hunter Colonel Rimfire is out to bag Cool Cat. Using Ella the mechanical elephant as camouflage, the tenacious hunter tracks the cat wherever he may be—the jungle, the circus, even a Paris racetrack. The Colonel (like Cool Cat, voiced by Larry Storch) blasted his way through four Cool Cat expeditions.

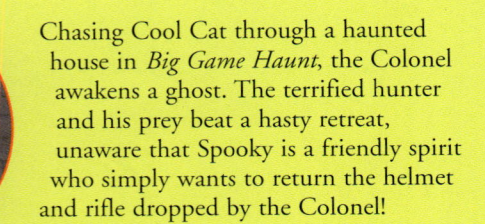

Chasing Cool Cat through a haunted house in *Big Game Haunt*, the Colonel awakens a ghost. The terrified hunter and his prey beat a hasty retreat, unaware that Spooky is a friendly spirit who simply wants to return the helmet and rifle dropped by the Colonel!

Cool Cat drives a groovy dune buggy.

Bartholomew

Robert McKimson directed a unique Merrie Melodie cartoon titled *Bartholomew Versus The Wheel*. In it, a little boy narrates the story of Bartholomew, a large dog with a grudge against wheels—all wheels. When the dog seizes the wheel of an airplane, it whisks him away on an adventure in the Sahara desert.

Bartholomew Versus The Wheel is rendered in a simplified art style reminiscent of James Thurber's drawings.

Bunny and Claude

"We Rob Carrot Patches" was the motto of jazz-era carrot thieves Bunny and Claude. This daring duo were pursued by the Sheriff through two cartoons. In *The Great Carrot Train Robbery* directed by Robert McKimson, they take over a locomotive—and drive everyone loco.

Nelly's Folly

Nelly the singing giraffe becomes a star when she moves to the big city in *Nelly's Folly*, directed by Chuck Jones. But an affair with a married giraffe leads to scandal, and Nelly returns to the jungle. There, she finds true love with her singing soul mate. Nominated for an Academy Award, this film has some of the most dazzling layouts ever designed by Maurice Noble (who receives a co-director credit with Abe Levitow).

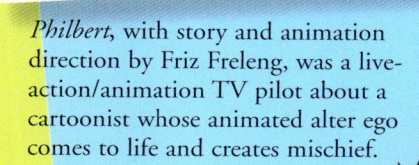

A vinyl Merlin The Magic Mouse doll made by Dakin

Zany characters

Looney Tunes directors never ceased to experiment with new concepts. Notable among them are Chuck Jones' two Oscar nominated cartoons *Now Hear This* and *High Note* about sound and music, and Alex Lovy's *Norman Normal*, a satire on social behavior.

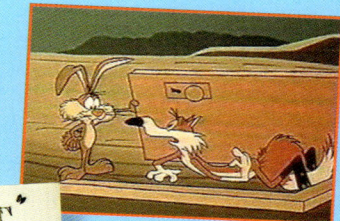

Speedy Rapid Rabbit debuted in Robert McKimson's *Rabbit Stew And Rabbits Too*.

Philbert, with story and animation direction by Friz Freleng, was a live-action/animation TV pilot about a cartoonist whose animated alter ego comes to life and creates mischief.

Roving Martian

In *Martian Through Georgia*, a neurotic alien is advised by his psychiatrist to travel, but after several antenna-raising adventures on Earth, decides to go home to a Martian girl who loves him.

The magic mouse

Merlin is a magician mouse with a voice that sounds like W.C. Fields. Accompanied by his sidekick, Second Banana, he gives magic shows and eludes hungry cats out west in the Ozark Mountains, and on stages all over the globe. Larry Storch provided Merlin's voice (though Daws Butler established the role in the first cartoon).

Merlin's magic hat is capable of producing anything from a turkey dinner to a spaceship!

SLAP HAPPY

WELCOME TO THE NOMINATIONS for the funniest slapstick routines in Looney Tunes. Slapstick has probably been around since one caveman watched and laughed as another caveman fell over. But slapstick today originated in vaudeville theater and was carried over to the days of silent movies. Of course, Warner Bros. cartoons and slapstick are inextricably linked. They go together like... well, like a cream pie and an unsuspecting face. May we hear a splat, please?

5 Slap dance

Bully For Bugs, directed by Chuck Jones, features a classic slapstick sequence. Bullfighter Bugs, wearing an oversized sombrero, dances up to the bull to the strains of the "Mexican Hat Dance." He lightly slaps the bull twice across the face, then zips away. The angered bull then dances up to Bugs, who slaps him again. Bugs twirls the sombrero in the air, dancing victoriously until he drops down his rabbit hole with the hat covering it. The bull comes up to the edge of the hat, which lifts up just enough for Bugs' hand to come out and slap the bull one last time.

4 The switcheroo

This sequence comes from *Rabbit Fire*, one of a trilogy of cartoons featuring Elmer Fudd as the baffled hunter who runs into two giants of slapstick: Bugs Bunny and Daffy Duck. The fun begins when the bunny and the mallard take turns to confuse the law-abiding Elmer as to whether it's rabbit hunting season or duck season. Bugs tacks up a sign that says "Duck Season Opens," whereupon Daffy dons a rabbit suit. Bugs enters in the duck outfit, so Daffy tells Elmer to shoot him, until we see the tree where the sign has now changed to "Rabbit Season Opens," causing Daffy to get blasted. One of the most brilliant aspects of this sequence is Mel Blanc's vocals of Bugs imitating Daffy and vice-versa.

Daffy's expression says it all: Why is the rabbit getting another *award?*

The humble Bunny brings home the gold once more—and finds the statue in-genius.

Award-winning bunny
Although Bugs is usually on the giving rather than receiving end of slapstick gags, he's created so many that we've awarded him this Wile E. Coyote "Slappy" award. Whether he's planting a big, wet kiss on someone's lips or tying a hunter's gun in a knot so he shoots himself, Bugs Bunny can always be called on to put the slap in slapstick.

3 Like it or lump it

When it comes to slapstick props, what's funnier than an oversized wooden mallet? TWO oversized wooden mallets. So, it follows that in order to increase the humor of one cartoon head bashing, you need to create a "whole lotta lumps." This is what Bugs sets out to achieve in the cartoon, *Rabbit's Kin*, directed by Robert McKimson. Pete Puma is the dumb beast who gets his stick slapped by the venerable Bunny. It isn't only that Pete falls for getting his head whacked once, he goes for a record three times. In the third round, he takes the mallet in his own paws and gives it to himself.

JUDGE'S HONORABLE MENTION

The weakest link....

Slapstick comedy often involves pain. In *The Ducksters*, a quiz program parody, Daffy the host punishes Elmer the contestant for incorrect answers. This includes TNT, a clobbering by a safe falling from the rafters, and drowning by 600 gallons of genuine Niagara Falls water.

Oversized mallet: In slapstick, bigger is better.

Pete has a mortal fear of lumpy gravy and lumpy oatmeal.

2 Duck and cover

Chuck Jones' *To Duck Or Not To Duck* contains a hilariously extended slapstick routine. When Elmer shoots Daffy out of the sky, the duck challenges him to a fair fight in a boxing arena (located right in the middle of the woods). First, Daffy rips off Elmer's clothes down to his underwear. Next, the duck referee demonstrates all the illegal boxing moves by poking, prodding, and jabbing Elmer: "None of this (PUNCH), or any of this (POW)." Daffy repeats the illegal moves to ensure Elmer understands. Every time Elmer's dog cheers his master or boos Daffy, he is pelted by a barrage of handy items thrown by the other duck spectators. Elmer finally gets even by repeating the illegal moves on Daffy and the referee.

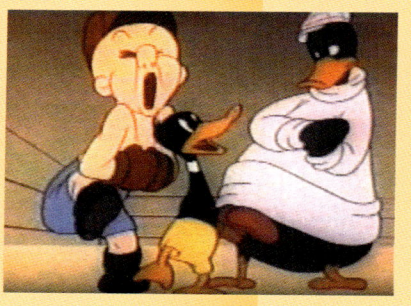

1 Double act

Our top choice for best slapstick gag comes from the classic cartoon *What's Up, Doc?*, directed by Robert McKimson. This is a tale of Bugs' fictional autobiography, looking at his foray into the vaudeville circuit. Vaudeville was a popular stage entertainment famous for its variety of short acts such as song-and-dance turns, juggling performances, and, of course, slapstick routines. In the cartoon, the out-of-work bunny teams up with popular entertainer Elmer Fudd to form a double act—their routine consists of bad jokes, the punchlines of which are accentuated by a stream of classic slapstick bits, including a pie in the face, pokes in the eyes, and seltzer squirted down the pants. It doesn't get any better than this!

Cream pies: not just for dessert!

Bugs with a giant wooden mallet again: He must keep the giant wooden mallet company in business.

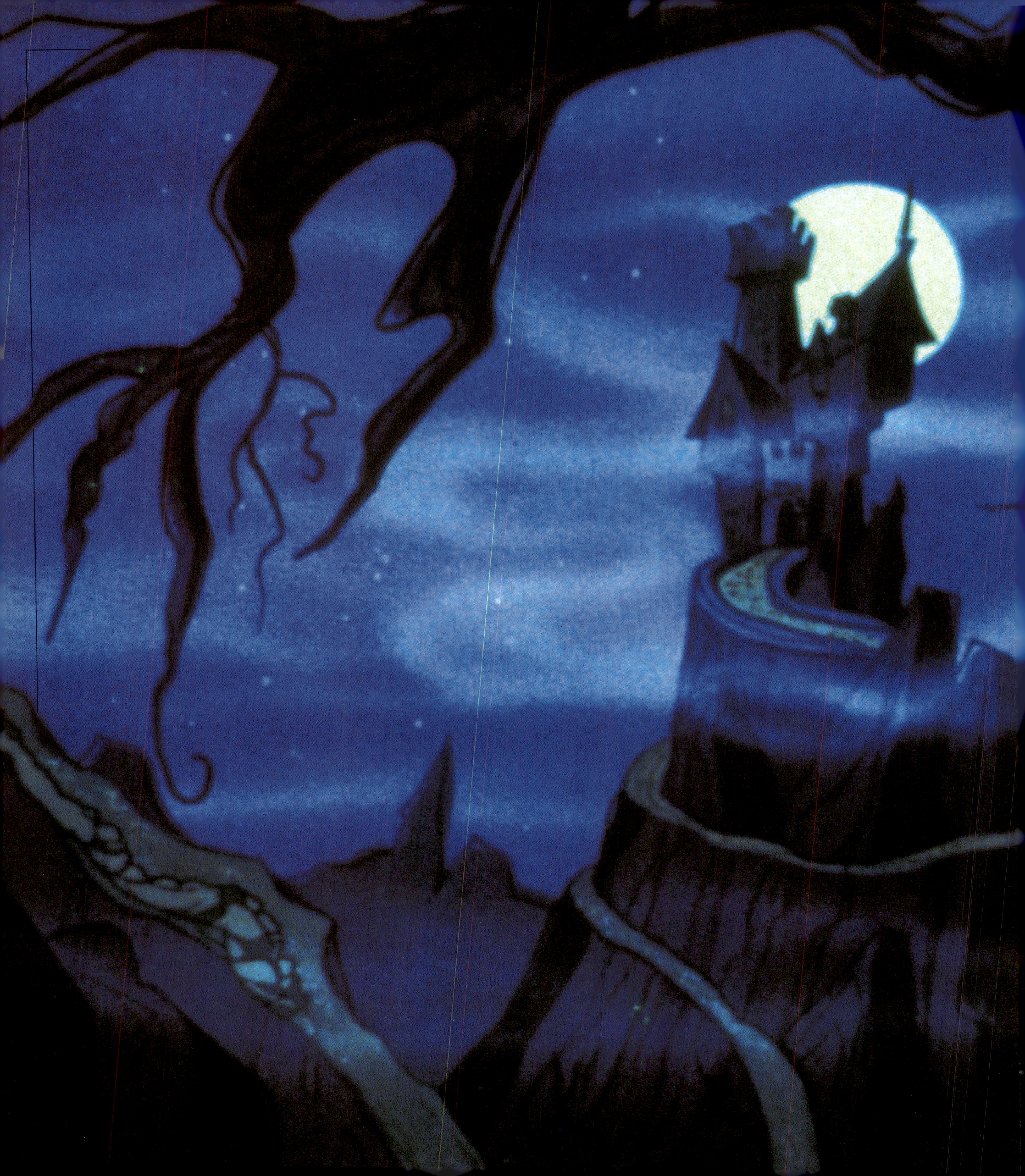

UNFORGETTABLE

WARNER BROS. had a genius for creating memorable cartoon characters. Even those who appeared in just one film or a handful of cartoons made an unforgettable mark on our consciousness. They are the beloved supporting stars: the gangsters, gremlins, singing frogs, mice, penguins, and daydreamers. What would Looney Tunes be without them?

SHOW STOPPERS

WE OFTEN THINK of the Looney Tunes gang as performers—they have all the skills of a great repertory company: snappy slapstick, manic melodrama, and vicious verbal gags. Two characters, however, stand out from the others as genuine stage performers. Enter singing, dancing Michigan J. Frog and baby mime Playboy Penguin.

Going for croak
In the Chuck Jones masterpiece, *One Froggy Evening*, a member of a wrecking crew looks inside the cornerstone of a demolished building and finds a frog in a box. Michigan J. Frog, released from his 50 years' entombment, demonstrates a most unfroglike ability to sing and dance.

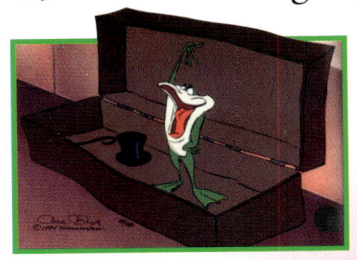

Do the Michigan
Michigan J. Frog's music repertoire features 1890s hits such as "Hello Ma Baby," "I'm Just Wild About Harry," and "Please Don't Talk About Me When I'm Gone." One song, "The Michigan Rag," was a faux-Nineties riff specially created for the cartoon.

"I'M JUST WILD ABOUT HARRY"

The box contains the cornerstone document along with the frog.

Trying to induce an encore. Flabby, ain't he? *Ribbit!*

Torpid toad
Alas, after his exuberant songs and dances, the frog reverts to lazy froghood. His new owner, dreaming of big money, considers this no big deal—at least at first.

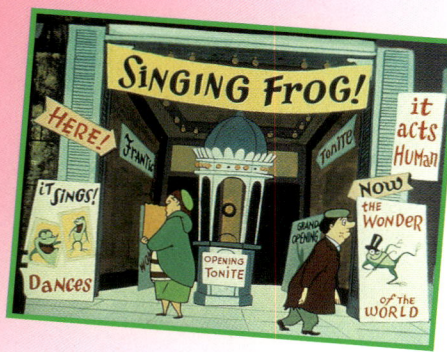

Voice of the frog
Singer, actor, and bandleader Bill Roberts was the singing voice for Michigan J. Frog in *One Froggy Evening*. Roberts' baritone voice was frequently heard in films such as *The Greatest Show On Earth* and he performed in small parts while under contract to MGM. According to studio records, when he recorded his tracks for Chuck Jones, the film was originally titled *It Hopped One Night*.

These humanlike arms turn into froggy flippers when the show is over.

Frog flop
In one theater after another, the fates conspire to prevent anyone other than Michigan's owner from seeing him in action. Finally, the now-destitute owner reburies the frog—for another would-be moneymaker (or T.V. network) to rediscover years later.

Little bird lost

When pantomime ice-skater Playboy Penguin gets lost in Brooklyn in *8-Ball Bunny*, Bugs offers to take him home. The continent-hopping trip is fraught with dangers including a hungry hobo who thinks "penguins is practically chickens!" At last, Bugs gets Playboy to the South Pole—only to find out that the penguin was really born in Hoboken, New Jersey.

A top hat six inches tall sounds small—but not if you're a penguin 10 inches tall.

Antarctic antics

In *Frigid Hare*, directed by Chuck Jones, the little penguin is a genuine South Pole dweller, with Bugs as an accidental tourist (after taking a wrong turn at Albuquerque). Reluctantly hanging around to babysit the silent bird, Bugs winds up protecting him from an uninvited third party.

Playboy's southern transportation in 8-Ball Bunny includes the steamship S. S. Admiral Byrd. There, Bugs finds the star performer debuting on the ship's menu.

Bugs turns royal performer in the Oscar-winning Knighty Knight Bugs—but a king's order transforms him from jester to jouster.

Giovanni Jones

In *Long Haired Hare*, Bugs Bunny's banjo, harp, and tuba playing disturb the precious eardrums of Giovanni Jones, opera singer. When the baritone batters the bunny allegro, our rabbit replies, "Of course you know this means war!" and a musical melee breaks out on stage.

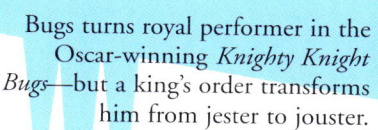

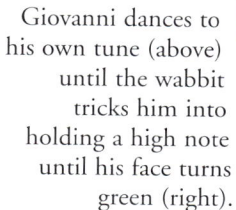

Giovanni dances to his own tune (above) until the wabbit tricks him into holding a high note until his face turns green (right).

In *Big Top Bunny*, Bugs is challenged by the jealous Bruno The Magnificent, the egotistical star of Colonel Corny's World Famous Circus. After being tricked on the trapeze act, the bunny gets even by blasting Bruno from a cannon.

Bugs tricks Bruno into taking a high dive from 5000 feet into a block of fresh cement.

MENACE TO SOCIETY

DAFFY, SYLVESTER, and the Looney Tunes gang are hardly upright citizens—far from it. They are famous for Looney larks and Merrie mischief that serves no one but themselves! But there is a big jump from ducks and puddy tats to the Tunes who are most out of tune—the really rotten criminals, monsters, and evildoers of our animated world. Here's a who's who of hoodlums, a rogues' gallery of gangsters, and a troop of true terrors!

Hatta Mari
Evil spy-bird, Hatta Mari, defeats the squadron woman-hater, Daffy Duck, in *Plane Daffy*. The se-duck-tress electrifies our hero with a kiss!

Rocky and Mugsy
Public enemies number one and two are Rocky and Mugsy, the pint-sized mob boss and his twenty-gallon sidekick. Rocky, strong and silent despite his short stature, has enough firepower in *Golden Yeggs* to scare Daffy into laying eggs for him—literally! Unfortunately for Rocky, his henchman Mugsy is as dumb as he is huge, and unwittingly spoils all his crooked capers.

A studio color model chart—not a police line-up.

Vampire Count Bloodcount, sets his sights—and fangs—on Bugs in *Transylvania 6-5000*. Unluckily for the bloodthirsty fiend, the rabbit gains the upper hand with a book of magic. Bugs' magic words change the bloodsucker from bat to human, over and over again, until the evil fiend is out for the count!

Claws for alarm

Crimestopper Bunny—ready to fast-talk brainy baddies...

Baby Faced Finster
In *Baby Buggy Bunny*, midget mafioso, Ant Hill Harry (a.k.a. Baby Face Finster), is disguised as a baby to hide himself—and his loot—from the police. Unfortunately for Finster, his buggy rolls down into Bugs Bunny's home and the diminutive gangster finds himself adopted by the rabbit. Bugs soon learns the truth about his little bundle of joy when he catches the baby shaving!

Bad habits like smoking send Finster to playpen prison.

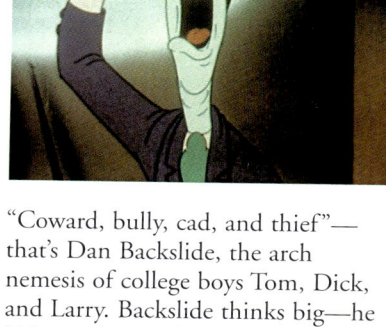

In *The Unmentionables*, Rocky's gang throw a party and end up with a very unwelcome guest. Agent Elegant Mess (Bugs Bunny) pops out from a birthday cake, disguised as a flapper, and shoots them with his carrot! Mess lures the mobsters into a breakfast cereal warehouse, where, after a run-in with the packing machine, the flakey felons are boxed up for jail!

"Coward, bully, cad, and thief"— that's Dan Backslide, the arch nemesis of college boys Tom, Dick, and Larry. Backslide thinks big—he kidnaps their girl, Dora Standpipe, standing by a tree, by stealing the tree.

Mr. Hyde

In *Hyde and Hare*, Bugs finds himself in the company of the kind and meek Doctor Jekyll but little does he know that things are about to change! After drinking a powerful potion, the Doc develops an evil alter ego—the fiendish Mr. Hyde. Bugs never quite realizes that the ax-wielding maniac is actually the Doc!

...but dumb ones will do.

The Crusher

As mascot to wrestler Ravishing Ronald in *Bunny Hugged*, Bugs doesn't want to see his boss pulverized by bad guy, the Crusher, and so tackles the big bruiser himself! He receives a beating at first, but, after dressing up as a tailor, Bugs leaves his opponent in stitches!

Slug McSlug

In *The Stupor Salesman*, gangster Slug McSlug is hiding from the police when salesman Daffy Duck pays him a visit. The villain clearly isn't interested, but Daffy won't give up until he's sold something, and offers him everything from brass knuckles and gun polish to bullets and bulletproof vests. Finally one of Daffy's lighters ignites the gas oven, blowing up McSlug's hideout!

Big, bad bully-dog Chester

Bulldog bad guys

The bulldog thug is a classic Looney enemy. Spike (left) gives doggy doings a bad name in *Tree For Two* and *Dr. Jerkyl's Hide*. In the latter, Spike loses his credibility when it appears that he's scared of a little cat (Sylvester), allowing sidekick Chester to take over. Similar embarrassment strikes Killer Diller (right) in Tex Avery's *Thugs With Dirty Mugs*, when an audience member rats on him to the boys in blue.

FELINE FRIENDS

COOL CATS, TOUGH TABBYS, and funny felines prowl their way through the back alleys and along the garden fences of Looney Tune-dom. Some appeared in a single film, while others, like Claude Cat, co-starred with multiple Looneys. If there's a puddy tat in the cartoon, it's sure to be a cat-tastrophy! But please note: any similarity between real cats, living or dead, is purely coincidental... and hilarious.

Little kitties
This pair of kitties appeared in the schoolroom romp, *I Haven't Got A Hat*, in which Little Kitty uncomfortably recites "Mary Had A Little Lamb." Beans, sometimes teamed with Porky Pig (Porky and Beans—get it?), gets even with snooty Oliver Owl just because the bird refuses to share his candy.

The self-proclaimed Hep Cat is more likely from Squaresville.

Ladies' cat
The Hep Cat sings about all the women who find him irresistible, but the only female feline he meets gives him the cold shoulder—indicated by an actual block of ice. He then proceeds to fall for a gal kitty—actually a puppet operated by a dog.

The night watch-cat
This little kitten fills in on kitchen guard duty when his father, Thomas Cat, is too sick to get out of bed. He gets picked on by a bunch of bully mice, but musters up some cat courage and takes them all on in the end.

Dazed and bruised—not an unusual state for the hapless Claude.

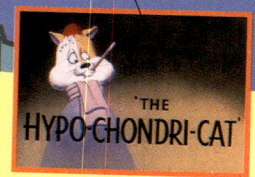

Hubie and Bertie take advantage of Claude's fear of illness in The Hypo-Chondri-Cat.

Unlucky cat
Claude is distinguished by a fine shock of red hair—although his body color changes from time to time. Poor Claude! No matter who he's up against, he always seems to get the worst of it. Whether it is with Hubie and Bertie in *Mouse Wreckers*, Marc Antony and Pussyfoot in *Feline Frame-up*, or Frisky Puppy in *Terrier Stricken*, Claude is always the punchline... or, rather, the punching bag.

In Terrier Stricken, Frisky Puppy drives Claude up the wall—literally. Every time the pooch has a sudden barking fit, Claude jumps!

Claude wills an angry bulldog to clobber him after he comes to believe he's lost the taste for mice (and therefore the will to live) in Cheese Chasers.

Conrad has a run-in with a chicken that pops out of a magician's hat in The Bird Came C.O.D.

Do the shuffle
Conrad is a likable character but the strangest looking cat you've ever seen. He has a funny shuffle walk and mostly reacts to whatever odd frustrating situation he finds himself in. His appearances include *The Bird Came C.O.D.*, *Porky's Café*, and *Conrad the Sailor*, all directed by Chuck Jones. In the latter, Conrad's voice is provided by famous voice actor Pinto Colvig.

Porky's furry fun

Porky is thrown out for the night by his three pussycats, including Sylvester, in *Kitty Kornered*. After suffering more trouble from Sylvester in *Claws For Alarm*, Porky went on to have further run-ins with annoying felines, including an alley cat who keeps him awake by singing on the backyard fence in *Notes to You*.

The lethargic star of *The Sour Puss* becomes a happy, grinning fellow when he dreams of a fish dinner!

Pizzicato Pussy Cat

A piano virtuoso mouse is caught by a cat, who in turn puts the mouse and his toy piano inside a real piano, then mimes that he's playing. The cat's owners think he's brilliant until the mouse's eyeglasses get broken and neither one of them can play anymore.

A layout drawing for Pizzicato Pussy Cat, labeled "Scene 15."

Lotsa luck... all bad

In *Early To Bet*, it's dog versus cat in various games of chance. When the cat loses at the roulette wheel or card table, the dog subjects him to a variety of painful penalties.

Little George and big, dumb Benny have the misfortune to attempt to chase after a mouse named Speedy Gonzales in *Cat-Tails for Two*.

Ouch! Who's back is Pussyfoot kneading? (Turn the page to find out....)

The cutest doggone Looney cat since Little Kitty—Pussyfoot.

These cats, who call themselves Captain and Snooks, are rivals for a sexy female feline in *Gruesome Twosome*.

In *Brave Little Bat*, Sniffles the Mouse only manages to escape from a cat with the help of his pal Batty, a talkative bat.

The cat's meow

The adorable little kitten Pussyfoot charms the pants off gruff Marc Antony, who turns out to be a softie at heart. In *Kiss Me Cat* (the title was inspired by the musical *Kiss Me Kate*), the dog has to teach his charge how to catch mice. This is no easy feat because the mouse repeatedly catches the cat!

CANINE CORPS

Bulldogs—the quintessential bully dogs!

DOGS PLAY AN IMPORTANT role in the Looney universe, if not always an intelligent one. They're bullies, guard dogs, and con artists. From major supporting players like Barnyard Dawg to the multitude of bit players, man's best friend is not always rabbit's best friend (or rooster's, or, especially, cat's). But one thing's for sure, crazy pooches such as emotionally needy Charlie Dog or sentimental Marc Antony, will never be forgotten.

Raised hackles from Pussyfoot claws.

Charlie Dog

Charlie just wants to find a new master. Someone to love and feed him. Trouble is, Charlie is a pest about it. In *Little Orphan Airedale*, he latches onto Porky Pig and annoys him, making Porky agree to let him stay. In the end, Porky drives off with Charlie chasing after the car.

One of Charlie's signature ploys is his sad, soulful routine, where his eyes grow large as saucers, making him look ultrasincere and vulnerable.

Rags McMutt escapes the dog pound. After hearing Charlie's story, he wants to get back in!

Marc Antony

The ferocious bulldog, Marc Antony, quickly turns into a bowl of mush at the sight of a cute little kitten, who, rather than being frightened, treats the dog's back as its own comfy, fur-lined bed. Marc Antony is superprotective of his little pet, whether this involves hiding her from his owner as in *Feed the Kitty* or going up against Claude Cat in *Feline Frame-Up*.

Marc Antony may have to bite through his lip to withstand the pain.

Marc Antony mistakenly thinks his Pussyfoot has been battered, beaten, and baked into a cookie. He puts the cookie on his back and sadly slumps away.

Spike and Chester

In *Tree For Two*, little Chester adores Spike until they go after Sylvester. Out of sight of Chester, Spike is mauled by an escaped black panther, which causes Chester to think that Spike cannot beat up a timid pussycat. In the end, Chester becomes Spike's hero.

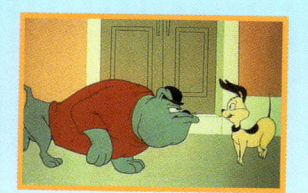

In *Dr. Jerkyl's Hyde*, Spike and Chester tackle a Sylvester monsterized by Dr. Jerkyl's formula.

Frisky puppy

As his name implies, Frisky Puppy likes to play. His favorite activity is sneaking up behind unsuspecting pussycats—particularly Claude—and barking for joy.

Willoughby and George

Of Fox and Hounds is a cartoon rewriting of John Steinbeck's *Of Mice and Men*, set during a hunt. George the fox keeps sending the dumb St. Bernard, Willoughby, on wild goose chases that result in him falling off a cliff.

Willoughby, THIS is the fox!

Russian around

The hot dog with the curly locks and Russian accent from *Hare Ribbin'* goes off in search of a "rabbit sand-a-wich." He gets more than he bargains for when he meets Bugs Bunny dressed as a mermaid: "This shouldn't happen to a dog!"

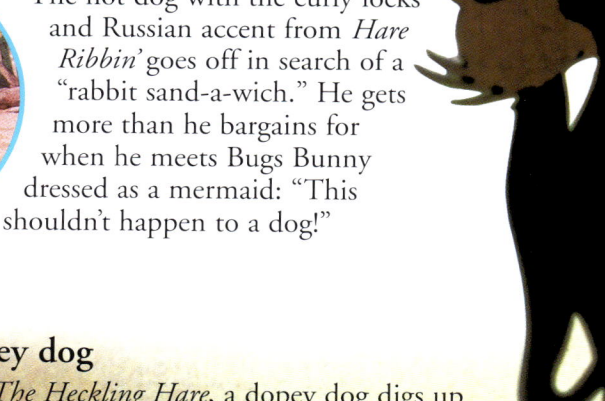

Dopey dog

In *The Heckling Hare*, a dopey dog digs up rabbit holes, but doesn't count on Bugs. When he digs an even bigger hole, possibly the longest screaming scene in all of Looneydom takes places between Bugs and the dumb dog.

The dog makes a return appearance in *An Itch In Time*, when a persistent flea won't leave him alone. He scratches so much that his owner, Elmer, threatens to give him a bath. Horrors!

The trials of being a dawg

Dogs chase cats and cats chase mice, right? Not always in the Looney Tunes world!

In *Double Chaser*, it's cat after mouse, dog after cat, then dog after mouse.

Did the cat become chicken? Nah! He was chicken all along.

Let us not forget the cat's best friend... the friendly neighborhood city dog catcher!

The poor doggy in *The Heckling Hare* weeps for the rabbit he thinks he's just squashed (actually it's a tomato placed in his paw by crafty Bugs).

101

CHEESE LOVERS

"EY, C'MERE!"

LOONEY TUNES MICE have to be especially clever and resourceful to get their daily cheese. But food is not their only concern. Some spend their days dodging hungry cats, while others get their kicks from driving innocent cats crazy. Mouse parents may find themselves raising huge babies of other animals—and vice versa. Whatever the situation, these madcap mice show a daring out of all proportion to their size!

Mel Blanc voiced Hubie.

"YEAH, YEAH. SURE, SURE!"

Stan Freberg was the voice of Bertie.

Hubie and Bertie
In their starring cartoons, all directed by Chuck Jones, clever Hubie and his dim pal Bertie usually aim to win themselves a home. Their schemes include tricking a naive cat into thinking he has gone crazy and, in *The Aristo-Cat*, convincing a pampered housecat that a bulldog is really the rodent he's meant to eat. In *House Hunting Mice*, the pair take on robots when they become squatters in a futuristic home.

Usually Hubie is brown and Bertie is gray, but sometimes it's the other way around. Bertie can be easily identified, however—he's the one with the giant buck teeth.

In Cheese Chasers, *the pair stuff themselves with enough cheese to last the average mouse 2,000 years!*

Life with Claude
Claude Cat is Hubie and Bertie's favorite victim. They delight in turning him into a quivering wreck with their mind games. In *Cheese Chasers* (left), the cat tries to figure out why the Hubie and Bertie have given up cheese and want to be caught. Claude later went on to become a solo star without the two mice.

Bertie needs instructions spelled out very clearly in The Hypo-Chrodri-Cat.

Miscellaneous mice

Mice appeared in Warner Bros. cartoons for many years before any single mouse became a star. In *The Cat Came Back* (left), a baby mouse and kitten become friends and unite their fighting families. Mice are sometimes villains, as in *Scaredy Cat* where Sylvester must save Porky from a haunted house full of killer mice.

An ear for music

A mouse upstages concert pianist Bugs Bunny in *Rhapsody Rabbit* by heckling the hare to the tune of "Hungarian Rhapsody No. 2." When noted film composer Erich Wolfgang Korngold saw the film he fell out of his chair laughing!

It's not Bugs who gets the standing ovation.

Mice, cats—and dogs

"The enemy of my enemy is my friend" is an old saying. Dogs, cats, and mice sometimes ally against a tough opponent, such as the master of the house. In *Feed The Kitty* (left) bulldog Marc Antony thinks kitten Pussyfoot is riding on his back—but it's really a mouse.

Mouse stars

Mice replace humans in rodent cartoon parodies of popular TV comedies The Honeymooners and The Jack Benny Show. In *The Mouse That Jack Built*, the actual cast of the latter show—Jack Benny, Eddie Anderson, Don Wilson, and Mary Livingston, along with Mel Blanc, who was a regular on Benny's show—voice the mousey characters themselves.

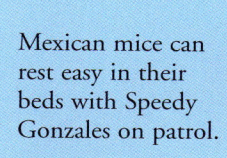

Sylvester Cat thinks a baby mouse is his son in *A Mouse Divided*.

Mexican mice can rest easy in their beds with Speedy Gonzales on patrol.

Mice fight against a cat dictator and his ratty spy in the World War II-set *5th Column Mouse*.

A hungry mouse in *Stooge for a Mouse* turns cat and dog friends into enemies.

In *The Mouse That Jack Built*, two mice are tricked into a cat's mouth disguised as a swanky night club. But the live-action ending shows Jack Benny waking from a catnap. It was all a dream!

Daws Butler voiced both Ralph and Morton in The Honey-Mousers.

Crafty cat-dodgers

The Honey-Mousers and its sequels parodied Jackie Gleason's popular sitcom *The Honeymooners*. Two mouse neighbors try a variety of creative ways to get past a cat to a food supply. In *Cheese It, The Cat*, one of their efforts involves riding on a flying champagne cork.

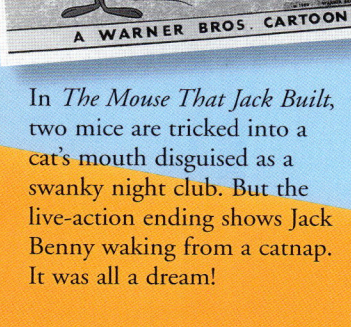

MINI-TOONS

THE STARS OF LOONEY TUNES are known for supersizing it. Be they rabbits, cats, or roosters, they're almost always drawn bigger and brassier than their real-life counterparts. This isn't always the case, however. Quite a few of Warner's Looney leading lights are little guys—but they still pack a powerful punch, proving that size isn't everything!

Home hunters
In *A Horse Fly Fleas*, A. Flea teams up with a homeless horsefly (literally a horse with wings) and together the try to set up home on a dog's back.

Seen close up, dog hairs become a forest.

Under the magnifying glass
A. Flea was a little blue-skinned bug whose home of choice in *An Itch In Time* was Elmer Fudd's pooch. Singing his catchy signature tune "There's Food Around the Corner," A. Flea gets out salt, pepper, and mustard and prepares his feast—a bunch of the dog's skin between two slices of bread. When the dog bites back, the bug utilizes mining equipment to make the most of his meat.

Batty's wings are his only batlike features.

Totally batty
The Brave Little Bat, directed by Chuck Jones, introduced Sniffles' motormouthed pal. The blabbering lighthouse keeper bat also appeared in many of the mouse's comic-book stories.

You need a magnifying glass to recognize A. Flea from inches away—but his victims' howls carry for miles.

Daydreamer
Ralph Phillips is the wild child whose highly imaginative adventures took place—surprise, surprise—in his imagination. The classics *From A To Z-Z-Z-Z* and *Boyhood Daze*, both directed by Chuck Jones, chronicle little Ralph's dreams of flight, Wild-West heroism, and more.

Mighty Angelo
After moving to a nice, quiet dog in the country, this circus-strongman flea must defend his hound homestead from a bully bulldog. The whole story's in *To Itch His Own*.

Angelo feels he's been working too hard at the circus.

Easter-egg kid
"I wanna Easter egg! I wanna Easter egg!" When Bugs stands in for a frazzled Easter Rabbit in *Easter Yeggs*, he quickly finds that the yolk's on him: A loudmouthed brat is out to shellshock egg-delivering bunnies with a handy hammer. Luckily, Bugs reroutes the rascal to mallet Elmer Fudd's egglike cranium instead.

Martian baby
Rocket-Bye Baby shows Mot the Martian infant's mistaken delivery to Earthling parents. The supersmart mini-alien perplexes Mr. and Mrs. Wilbur by doing income tax and using blocks to spell $E=MC^2$, while Mot's Earth equivalent, Yob, is misplaced on Mars.

Gambling Bug
In *Early To Bet*, a dapper beetle forces a cat to engage in games of chance with bulldog Hector by biting him. Alas, winning is never on the cards for the feline, who receives a painful punishment from Hector each time he loses. When the dog feels sorry for the cat and refuses to play on, the Gambling Bug himself steps in—and loses!

Chicks versus weasel
The Weasel himself isn't small—but his sweetly sneaky chick victim certainly is. The little chick figures a cure for his cold from "Dr." Weasel is worse than the disease. Chick's ultimate defense: passing his germs weaselward—AH-CHOO!

The chick caught a cold from staying out in a rainstorm.

Stan Freberg voiced the Gambling Bug.

BEFORE COLOR

WHEN SILENT MOVIES became talkies, musical shorts became a staple of every movie program. With the success of Disney's Mickey Mouse and Silly Symphonies, Warner Bros. decided to make their own series of musical cartoons, which would promote songs owned by Warners' music companies. Ex-Disney animators Hugh Harman and Rudolph Ising brought their character Bosko, the "Talk-Ink Kid," to Warner Bros.—and the Looney Tunes were born.

Bosko ended each cartoon by saying, "So long, folks!"

Bosko's falsetto voice was provided by cartoonist Johnny Murray. He took over the role from animator Carmen "Max" Maxwell, who worked on the pilot reel and the first release, Sinkin' In The Bathtub.

Bosko's uniform: big black boots, white gloves, and a derby hat!

Bosko and Bruno

Harman and Ising's answers to Mickey Mouse and Pluto were Bosko and his dog Bruno. Bosko was the all-singing, all-dancing, all-talking superstar of the first lively, upbeat Looney Tunes. The formula was simple: carefree Bosko would cavort about, having misadventures and playing music on any available object. To Depression-era audiences, he was the antidote to people's blues.

Bosko was often joined by his girlfriend, Honey, and her nephew, Wilber. The characters in the early cartoons moved in time to the musical soundtrack, supplied by a female trio, The Rhythmettes (who also voiced female characters), and a male quartet called The King's Men.

Piggy and Fluffy on their backfiring motorcycle in You Don't Know What You're Doin'

Foxy and Roxy

While the Looney Tunes series was dedicated to the antics of a recurring character, a second series of cartoons, Merrie Melodies, was created to feature miscellaneous characters. Foxy and Roxy appeared in the first Merrie Melodies. Foxy played a traffic cop, a trolley conductor, and a Mexican caballero in his few screen appearances. Roxy would arrive to sing a song and play the mandolin or piano—or even her dog's teeth!

Foxy in the second Merrie Melody, One More Time

Roxy in the first Merrie Melody, Lady Play Your Mandolin

Piggy and Fluffy

The short-lived characters Piggy and Fluffy appeared in a pair of Merrie Melodies, although neither character became as popular as Bosko. Their first appearance, *You Don't Know What You're Doin'*, features red-hot jazz, a wild storyline, and a truly surreal visual style—elements that would come to define the Warner Bros. cartoons.

Goopy Geer

Goopy Geer was another of Warner Bros.' attempts to create a new recurring character for the Merrie Melodies. A lanky, loose-limbed dog, Goopy starred in a small number of cartoons. In the film entitled *Goopy Geer*, he plays piano in a rowdy night club and inspires everyone (and everything) to dance. In *Moonlight For Two*, Goopy is upstaged by a dancing stove, who ends up saving him from the baddie!

Each early Merrie Melody featured new characters and a new song. *I Wish I Had Wings* (above) had an all-bird cast, while *A Great Big Bunch Of You* is set in a junkyard. *Shuffle Off To Buffalo* takes place in heaven and *We're In The Money* sees a department store come to life!

Prohibition ends in Buddy's Beer Garden.

Goopy and his gal in Moonlight For Two

Buddy with his girlfriend Cookie and Towser the dog

Buddy

When Harman and Ising ended their contract with Warner Bros., the company replaced Bosko with Buddy, a happy-go-lucky young man whose exploits were simple and lighthearted. The Looney Tunes that featured him were either musical (as in *Buddy's Show Boat*) or mini-adventures (as in *Buddy's Lost World*). Neither format, however, could compete against the stronger personalities being created at the other studios, such as Donald Duck or Popeye. It would take a certain stuttering pig to become the first fully fledged Looney Tunes star a few years later.

Director Bernard Brown first voiced Buddy. Then animator Jack Carr stepped in, until child actor Jackie Morrow established the role.

The young animators

Leon Schlesinger fostered a hands-off approach to the new animation department, allowing his cartoonists to develop their own styles and try out new ideas. "We were grotesquely young, our eyes wide and unembarrassed by knowledge, wisdom, or theory, and hopelessly uncluttered by tradition or precedent," said Chuck Jones. "We lived and worked in an atmosphere of no restriction. Anything was possible, everything probable."

Hugh Harman (top) and Rudolph Ising (bottom) originally worked with Walt Disney in Missouri. Later, they joined him in Los Angeles. When they found themselves out of work, they produced the first Bosko short as a pilot. This cartoon was one of the first to feature synchronized speech.

The two animators' names produced the melodious-sounding "Harmon-Ising" partnership!

The animators worked in a run-down bungalow, which they affectionately nicknamed "Termite Terrace." It was a "little shack over on the Sunset lot," recalled Tex Avery. He described it as an "old dressing room or toilet or something, a little cottage sort of thing."

An evil, dancing skeleton leaps out of its grave in Hittin' The Trail To Hallelujah Land.

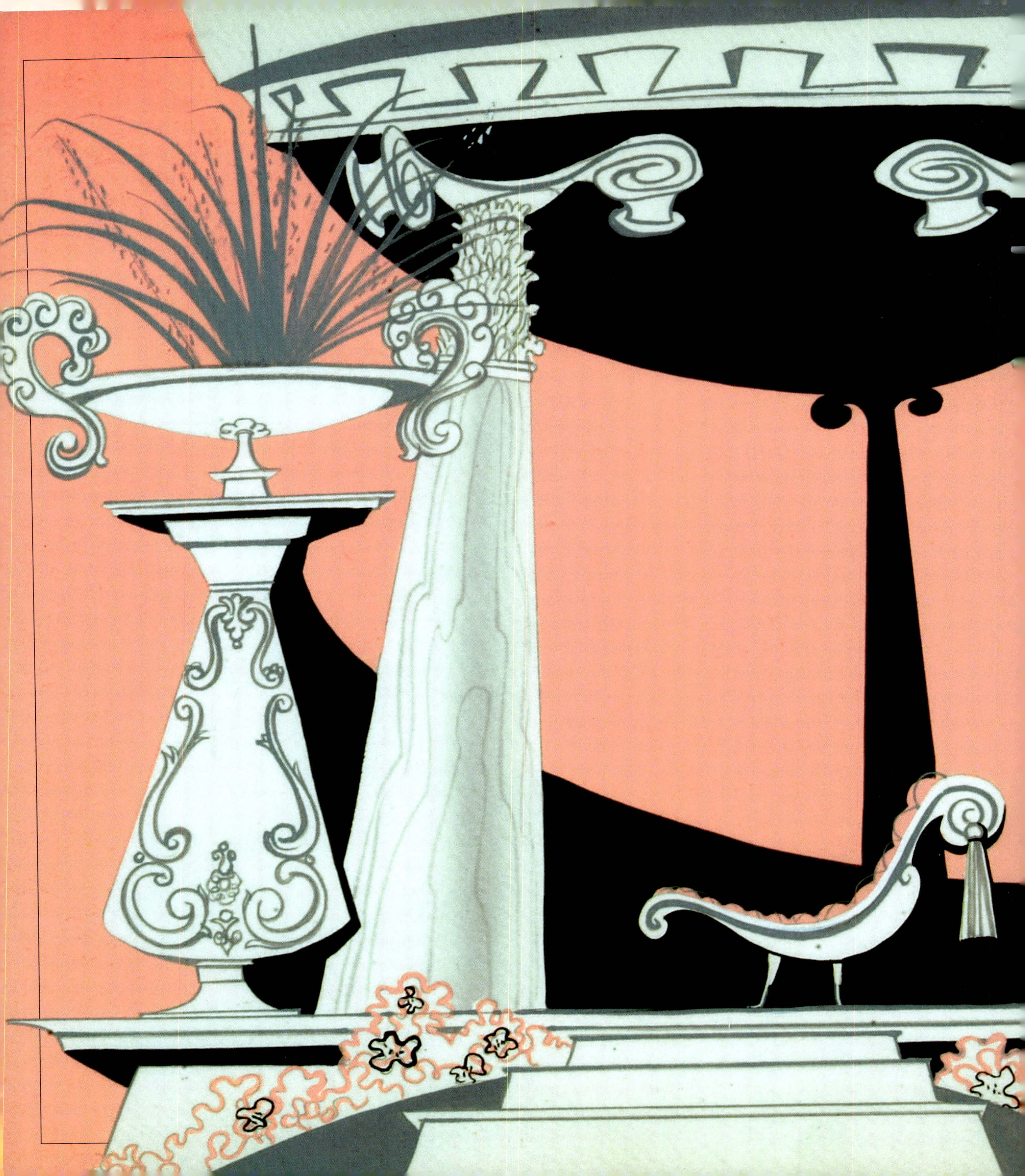

ANIMATED WORLD

A STAGGERING ARRAY of talented individuals worked at the Warner Bros. animation studio. These artists, writers, directors, musicians, and voices put the "looney" into Looney Tunes and became some of the most legendary names in cartoon history. They created a studio with a singular, original vision for animated cartoons—and classic characters that will live forever.

CARTOON MAKERS

The classic Looney Tunes were created at Warner Bros. studios in Burbank.

THE PEOPLE BEHIND the screen credits—the artists, writers, directors, and animators—were the heart and soul of the studio. They did more than make the characters move: they gave them personalities, attitude, and life. The creative teams developed the characters that came to define Looney Tunes: rapid-fire pacing, street-smart attitude, and daring outrageousness. These people, quite literally, *were* the Looney Tunes!

The goal of the cartoon makers—animation drawings that make people laugh.

Animating principles

The animators came from diverse backgrounds, but shared the desire to create the funniest cartoons ever made. Their skillful drawings, sense of humor, and sheer hard work will live forever—as long as "What's up, Doc?", "I Taut I Taw A Puddy Tat," and "That's All Folks!" are part of our common lexicon.

Friz Freling
Senior Director Isadore "Friz" Freleng worked for Walt Disney before he became head animator for directors Hugh Harman and Rudolf Ising at Warner Bros. He specialized in Tweety and Sylvester films and won Oscars for Bugs and Speedy cartoons. His trademarks include the masterful matching of music to comic action and the finely judged building of a gag toward a big payoff.

Chuck Jones
Chuck Jones directed some of the most well-known and celebrated Looney Tunes. His style evolved from the gentle cartoons featuring Sniffles to the fast-paced, action-packed Road Runner and Wile E. Coyote chases. Jones' approach was to look for humor in the details. Under his guidance, Bugs Bunny, Daffy Duck, and Porky Pig appeared in some of their defining cartoons, and he made superstars of Marvin the Martian, Michigan J. Frog, Charlie Dog, and Witch Hazel.

Jones won an Oscar for the Pepe Le Pew film *For Scent-Imental Reasons*, and accolades for such masterpieces as *What's Opera, Doc?*, *Duck Amuck*, and *Duck Dodgers In The 24 1/2th Century*.

Bob Clampett

Welcome to wackyland—Bob Clampett was Warner Bros.' zaniest director, whose way-out films literally stretched, squashed, and bounced the boundaries of animation.

Bob Clampett (center, with Bugs Bunny model) poses with his animators outside the studio.

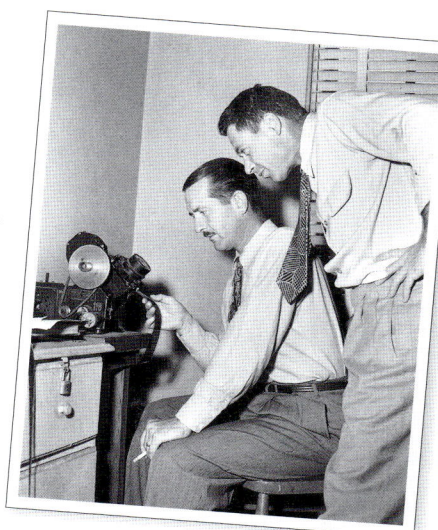

Back row, left to right: animator Elmer Wait, director Frank Tashlin, animator Larry Martin, and music writer Bernard Brown.
Front row, left to right: animator Sid Sutherland, Chuck Jones, Tex Avery.

Robert McKimson

One of the best animators of all time, Robert McKimson (seated, with animator Rod Scribner, right) became one of the mainstays of Warner Bros. cartoons when he was promoted into the director's chair. He specialized in directing Foghorn Leghorn, Tasmanian Devil, and Speedy Gonzales, and, with Freleng and Jones, was one of the top directors of Bugs Bunny and Daffy Duck cartoons.

The writers

At Warner Bros. Animation, the writers also had to be cartoonists. They used pens and pencils to write and draw comic strips, which the directors, animators, layout, and background artists turned into cartoons. Tedd Pierce (above left) worked with Chuck Jones and Robert McKimson, and was responsible for Pepe Le Pew in *Odor-Able Kitty* and Speedy Gonzales in *Cat-Tails For Two*. Warren Foster (right) worked on Tweety in *A Tale Of Two Kitties* and Foghorn Leghorn in *Walky Talky Hawky*.

Tex Avery

Tex Avery directed many of the films people most associate with the zany Warner Bros. style. He constantly defied cartoon conventions, pioneering such innovations as breaking the fourth wall (addressing the audience), the exaggerated double-take (for example, bulging eyes), and parodies of contemporary newsreels and travelogs. His work with Bugs and Daffy is greatly celebrated and many of his one-shots like *I Love To Singa* and *Page Miss Glory* have become cult classics.

Tex Avery's burgeoning visual imagination is displayed in a diary he made during a cross country trip as a young man. Filled with his own sketches and photographs, it is a fascinating insight into the mind of the artist.

VOICES AND MUSIC

LOONEY TUNES SOUNDTRACKS are as memorable to our ears as the animated visuals are to our eyes. The witty dialog, madcap musical cues, and vast array of crashes, explosions, and "beep-beeps!" were produced by a small troop of talented actors and musicians, who matched every zany character and visual situation the artists could conjure.

Mel Blanc often lent his talents to children's records featuring the Looney Tunes stars.

Mel Blanc

Mel Blanc was known as "the man of a thousand voices," roughly half of which were for characters in Warner Bros. cartoons: Bugs Bunny, Daffy Duck, Porky Pig, Foghorn Leghorn, Tweety, Sylvester... the list goes on and on. His voice so defined the Warner cartoon sound, he was signed to a long-term contract and received voice-talent credit for most of his animation career.

Mel Blanc records his lines for director Robert McKimson.

Mel Blanc was given a "Golden Carrot" award by the staff of Warner Bros. animation for his years of service. Ironically Blanc was allergic to carrots and had to have a bucket standing by during recordings, so after every take of "Ehh... what's up, Doc?" he could spit the carrots out of his mouth.

Speechless

In 1961, Blanc was in a coma for three weeks after a car accident. Each day, his doctor would ask him how he was, with no response. One day he asked, "How are you feeling today, Bugs Bunny?" Blanc answered back in Bugs' voice, "Ehh, just fine, Doc. How are you?" Mel recovered from his injuries, but spent the next seven months recording Looney Tunes in a full body cast!

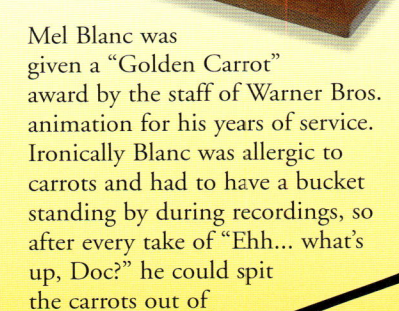

"EHH... WHAT'S UP, DOC?"

Musical notes

Chuck Jones directed many cartoons with music as the subject, notably the Academy Award-nominated *High Note*. This film takes place on a sheet of music, with the notes as characters who come to life (right).

Stan Freberg

Best known as an actor and satirist, Stan Freberg was a regular voice in Warner Bros. cartoons. His most famous characterizations were those of Junyer Bear, Pete Puma, and the musical Three Little Bops—the latter cartoon garnering him his only on-screen credit. He was the Goofy Gophers (both Mac *and* Tosh), one half of mice duo Hubie and Bertie, and Chester to Mel Blanc's Spike.

June Foray

Actress June Foray won the hearts of Looney Tunes fans for her vocal portrayal of Granny in many Tweety cartoons and subsequent television series and specials. She was also the voice of the mischievous Witch Hazel in the Bugs Bunny films and worked frequently on Looney Tunes in a variety of supporting roles: as Alice in *The Honey-Mousers*, Yosemite Sam's shrewish wife in *Honey's Money*, and Miss Prissy in *A Broken Leghorn*, to name but a few.

Arthur Q. Bryan

Arthur Q. Bryan voiced Elmer Fudd, one of the few major Looney Tunes stars not vocalized by Mel Blanc. Bryan had perfected the voice on a radio program called "The Grouch Club," as a character known as "The Little Man." Bryan had a prolific career as a comic actor on radio and television, but regularly played Fudd until his death in 1959. He occasionally portrayed other roles for Warner Bros. cartoons, but it's his Fudd that will live forever in the popular imagination.

Fudd's personality was influenced by Bryan's distinctive comic voice.

Looney Tunes writer Warren Foster wrote many songs based on the Warner Bros. cartoons, which were released on records and as sheet music (below).

Sheet music of a Daffy Duck song written for a children's record

Carl Stalling

Carl Stalling's musical scores have become synonymous with the sound of Warner Bros. cartoons. His ability to match frantic action to appropriate melodies—mixing his original scores with themes from classical music and contemporary popular tunes—has won him legions of admirers, while his knowledge of jazz turned obscure music into cartoon standards. Stalling's career began as a theater organist in Kansas City, Missouri. After moving to Hollywood, he joined Warner Bros. and remained there for over 20 years.

Stalling wrote scores for more than 500 Looney Tunes.

Raymond Scott

Composer and bandleader Raymond Scott's eccentric jazz was perfect music for cartoons, used for chase scenes and dramatic moments. His "Dinner Music For A Pack of Hungry Cannibals," for example, became the score for the jungle chase in Bugs Bunny's *Gorilla My Dreams*.

BACKGROUND ART

BACKGROUND SET ART, meticulously designed and painted by the layout artists, places the action of the story in locations that enhance the foreground action. These sets were never meant to be seen separately from the celluloid characters who appeared in front of them, but they are nevertheless true works of art and the artists who created them were masters of their field.

Layout drawing by Maurice Noble for a panoramic background in Rabbit Seasoning.

Early backgrounds

The earliest cartoons, produced in black and white, relied on simple, basic settings rendered in gray tones. Bosko, Buddy, and Beans bounced around in these early epics without having to worry about turning red with anger, green with envy, or plaid with color confusion.

Surreal situations, as in Porky In Wackyland *called for Dali-esque settings.*

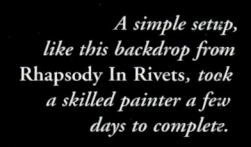

Layout artists work with the director to design the backgrounds for each shot in the film. They determine how and where the character will move through the scene. Notable layout artists at Warner Bros. include Hawley Pratt, Robert Givens, Pete Alvarado, Robert Gribbroek, and Maurice Noble.

A simple setup, like this backdrop from Rhapsody In Rivets, *took a skilled painter a few days to complete.*

Realistic backgrounds

Initially, Looney Tunes cartoons featured background scenes that were quite literal and realistic. Trees looked like real trees, the skies were bright blue, and boulders felt like real rocks. This gave the characters a foothold in reality, and made it easier for audiences to identify with the places and situations presented.

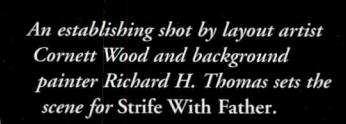

A mad scientist's lab from Birth Of A Notion *leaves plenty of room for the characters to act.*

An establishing shot by layout artist Cornett Wood and background painter Richard H. Thomas sets the scene for Strife With Father.

Philip De Guard's Brooklyn Bridge from Bowery Bugs.

Maurice Noble produced this concept painting for Zoom And Bored.

Noble's stylized jungle featured in Boyhood Daze.

Keeping it unreal

Over time, Warner Bros. animations began to feature sparser, less realistic background settings. Surreal space landscapes by Maurice Noble, abstract Tasmanian jungles by Richard H. Thomas, and simple Mexican mouse traps by Tom O'Loughlin were stylish and contemporary.

Heroic design

Each cartoon demanded between 30 and 50 backgrounds, which had to be produced at great speed. Background artists are the true heroes of animated cartoons. Richard H. Thomas, Paul Julian, Irv Wyner, Tom O'Loughlin, and Philip De Guard (right) are among Warners' best.

Rocket Squad *featured layouts by Ernie Nordli and background art by Philip De Guard.*

Paul Julian painted this nautical background for Mutiny On The Bunny.

Philip De Guard adopts a more abstract style in Bewitched Bunny.

A dynamite Richard H. Thomas set from The Oily American.

Bunny Hugged *featured background art by Philip De Guard and layouts by Pete Alvarado.*

115

SUPPORTING FEATURES

ONCE UPON A TIME, before The Bugs Bunny Show and Cartoon Network, Looney Tunes and Merrie Melodies shorts were shown in theaters as part of the moviegoing experience. It was in darkened movie theaters that they made their first impressions on the public and became the most popular cartoons in the world. Appreciated by adults and adored by children, the Looney Tunes are motion-picture classics.

Lobby cards

To publicize each cartoon, special pieces of art were created by the cartoon staff for use by theater owners—to be distributed as a form of stills photos or affixed to one-sheet lobby posters. These pieces are also referred to as "lobby cards" because they are designed to displayed in theater lobbies. They were also used to promote new Looney Tunes in magazines and newspapers.

A lobby board on display outside a movie theater

Classic cartoons

Looney Tunes and Merrie Melodies are famous all around the world, as shown by this promotional poster from Spain. Even before the cartoons appeared regularly on television, movie audiences cherished them.

The best place to see a Looney Tunes or Merrie Melodies cartoon—on the "silver screen."

The best promotional art captured the attitudes of the cartoon's characters in a single illustration.

Theater cartoons

Many Looney Tunes cartoons contain references to their original presentation in movie theaters. A silhouette of a noisy movie patron returning to his seat—who is addressed by the cartoon's hero—fooled many theater audiences in *Daffy Duck And Egghead*. In *Cinderella Meets Fella*, Cindy meets her Prince Charming at the very theater showing the cartoon they are in!

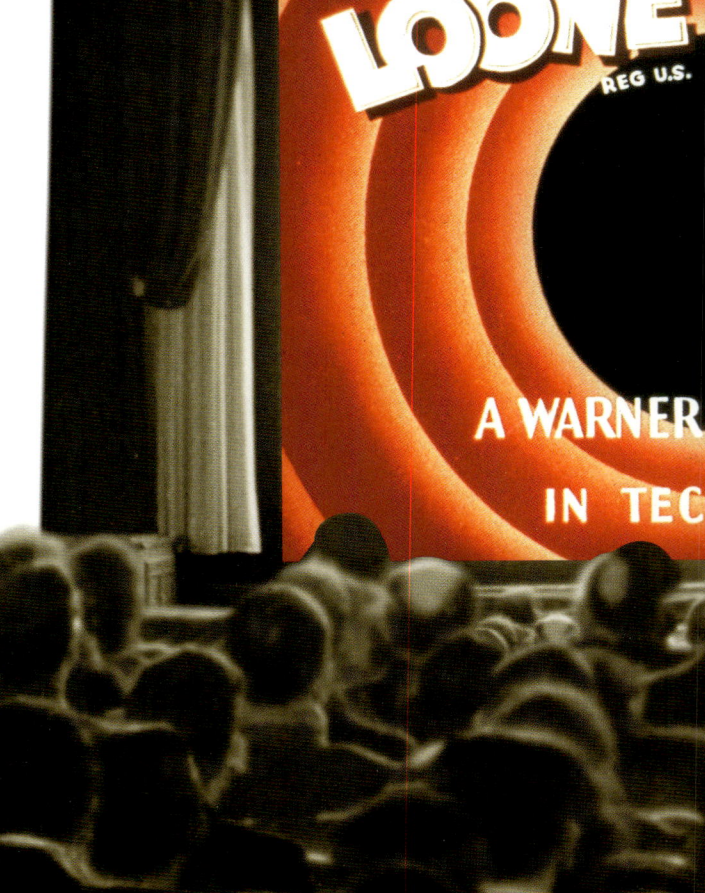

In *People Are Bunny*, Bugs poses as a theater usher to misdirect Daffy.

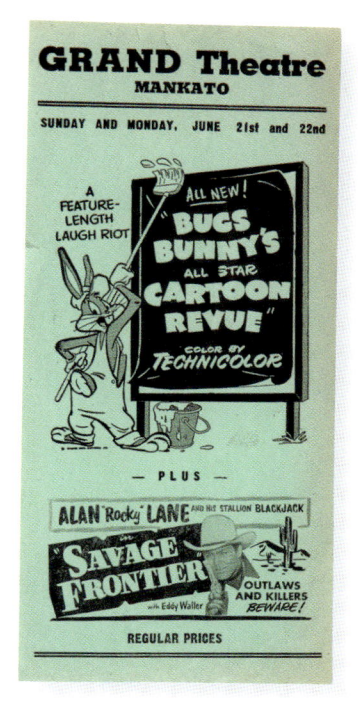

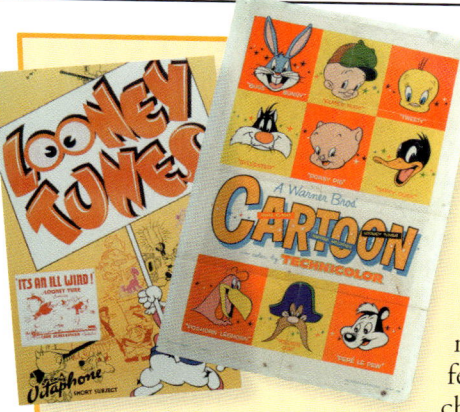

Posters

During their original theatrical runs, full-color posters were created to promote the showing of Looney Tunes and Merrie Melodies cartoons. These movie posters usually featured the most popular characters (especially Bugs, Daffy, and Porky) in a generic scene or design that could be used to promote any latest release—the specific cartoon was indicated by a lobby card stuck onto the poster, such as the Chuck Jones one-shot *Eager Beaver* (right). The current scarcity of these colorful pieces has made them highly sought-after collectibles.

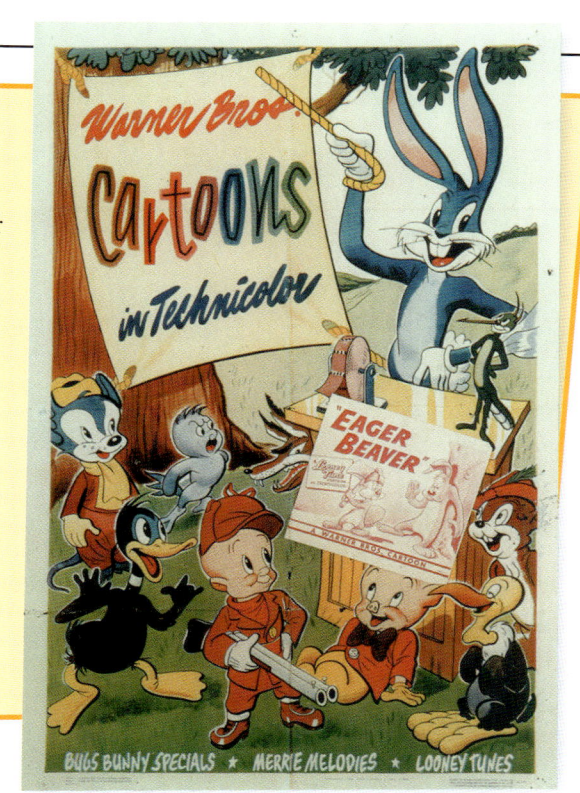

Full-length features

Compilation programs of shorts were shown in theaters as feature films. In later years, new bridging material was added to link the older cartoon footage together, as in *The Bugs Bunny Road Runner Movie*, directed by Chuck Jones.

Print advertisements

Warner Bros. created promotional line art for print ads so movie patrons wouldn't miss their favorite Looney Tunes star. Additional publicity was created when the Academy of Motion Picture Arts and Sciences nominated the cartoons for Oscars. Looney Tunes and Merrie Melodies won a total of six Oscars, including one for Best Documentary Short for *So Much For So Little* directed by Chuck Jones.

Daffy believes his own hype in a print advert.

A Looney Tune was part of every performance.

Theater bills

Animated cartoons were an essential part of every film show, with programs sometimes changing three times a week. Looney Tunes cartoons played their first run in theaters owned by Warner Bros. and were then shown in independent theaters for up to a year. Audiences generally only saw each cartoon once.

THE MAKING OF A CLASSIC

CHUCK JONES' MAGNUM OPUS, *What's Opera Doc?*, is the ultimate Bugs Bunny-Elmer Fudd musical spoof and a seven-minute masterpiece that defines the entire concept of Looney Tunes. Jones worked with a talented team that included writer Michael Maltese, layout artist Maurice Noble, musical director Milt Franklyn, and voice artists Mel Blanc and Arthur Q. Bryan. A look at the making of this classic shows the processes that all Warner Bros. cartoons went through to reach the screen.

What's Opera, Doc? was selected for the National Film Register, which ensures the preservation of films that are "culturally, historically, or aesthetically significant."

Reinventing the formula

What's Opera, Doc? relocates the simple rabbit-hunt formula to the epic setting of a Wagnerian opera. Armed with his "spear and magic helmet" instead of a rifle, Fudd commands the elements to stake his prey. Bugs tricks him into a duet, disguising himself as a beautiful Viking girl, Brunhilde. When Elmer discovers the ruse, he destroys the bunny but regrets it afterward. As Bugs quips at the end: "What did you expect from an opera—a happy ending?"

Writer Michael Maltese produced these original story sketches for *What's Opera, Doc?*

Once again, Bugs dresses as a woman to woo Fudd away from his weapon.

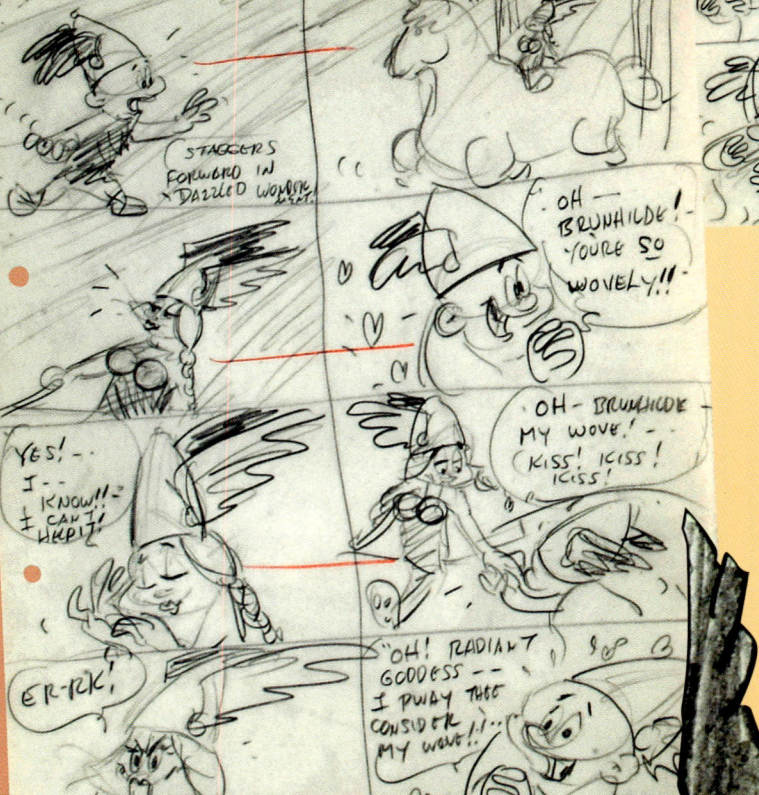

Storyboards

Every cartoon started with an idea from either the staff storymen or the director. The storyman, in this case Michael Maltese, drew the entire cartoon in panels, like a comic book, and submitted it to the director for approval. The storyman and director then revised the storyboards.

The opening sequence of the huge, dark shadow directing the storm was a tribute to Bill Tytla's animation in the *Night on Bald Mountain* section of Disney's *Fantasia*.

Chuck Jones' pencil sketches capture the drama and simplicity of line that are hallmarks of this great cartoon.

Story meeting

When the story sketches were completed, they were pinned to a large board, and this became the blueprint for the animated cartoon. The entire staff—directors and animators from every unit—were invited to pitch additional gags in a jam session called the "Yes Session." This was named for the fact that no one could say "no" to any idea. After this meeting, the dialog was typed up and recorded.

Richard Wagner

In the early 20th century, Richard Wagner (1813-1883) was the most famous operatic composer in America. He is celebrated for his "music dramas"—operas in which he aimed to perfectly fuse words, music, and stagecraft. This approach is seen in his famous series of operas based on German myths, *The Ring* (*The Rhinegold, The Valkyrie, Siegfried,* and *Twilight of the Gods*). The characters in *What's Opera, Doc?* are parodies of those from *The Ring*: the hero Siegfried and the woman he loves, the goddess-turned mortal Brunhilde.

Making time

Every cartoon passed through a number of departments—layout, background, animation, ink, and paint—before the cels were filmed (right). The unusually complex *What's Opera, Doc?* required longer than usual in each department. Jones had the staff mark the additional time to Road Runner productions, which he knew could be produced on shorter schedules!

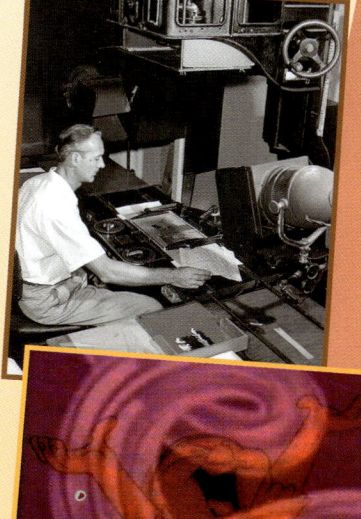

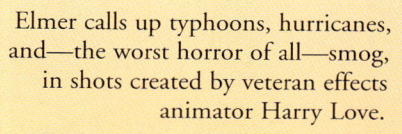

Elmer calls up typhoons, hurricanes, and—the worst horror of all—smog, in shots created by veteran effects animator Harry Love.

Animation drawings

After the voices were recorded, the animators used the timed soundtrack (written on a chart called an "exposure sheet") to guide them as to the number of drawings required in each scene. The animators looked at Jones' layout drawings—and the action indicated on the storyboards—to make the pictures that made the characters appear to move. For each second of film, they drew between 12 and 24 pencil animation drawings.

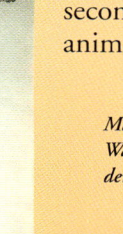

Registration holes fit in pegs on the artists' desks.

Magic helmet, Wagnerian demigod-style!

What's Opera Doc? used the vocal talents of Mel Blanc as Bugs and Arthur Q. Bryan as Elmer. On the original vocal track, Bryan yelled the line "Smog!," but Blanc, who could yell like no one else, rerecorded that one word for Elmer.

ANIMATED STARS

POKING FUN AT Hollywood was a Looney Tunes tradition. Without doubt, the animators were inspired by screen comedians such as Charlie Chaplin, Buster Keaton, and W.C. Fields. But their close proximity to then-contemporary film stars, by virtue of being on Warner Bros. main lot, gave the cartoonists the opportunity to lampoon the personalities, visual characteristics, and famous roles of Hollywood's greatest.

Smoldering star
In Bob Clampett's *Bacall To Arms*, a wolf goes to the movies and dozes right through—until Laurie Becool (a cartoon version of Lauren Bacall) appears and drives him wild with her sexy stare.

Bugs Marx the spot
Bugs Bunny has been compared to all three of the subversive Marx Brothers—Groucho in particular. Bugs' line, "Of course you know, this means war!", was originally spoken by Groucho in the 1933 Marx Brothers movie *Duck Soup*. The wabbit himself donned a Groucho disguise in *Slick Hare* and *Wideo Wabbit*.

Just like Groucho's, Bugs' eyebrows are painted on.

Bugs with Groucho trademark mustache and cigar... er, carrot

Bugs usually has good dress sense, but in this case he's made an exception.

Frankly my dear...
Clark Gable was the king of Hollywood leading men. Vocal mimic Kent Rogers parodied Gable's voice in Avery's *Hollywood Steps Out*, where the movie hunk is chasing a blonde—who in the end turns out to be Groucho in drag! Ouch!

Groucho club
Tex Avery compared Bugs Bunny to the cigar-chomping, fast-talking Marx brother: "You should visualize him as Groucho Marx. If he ever runs from anyone, he has a trick in mind. If you look back at the old Grouchos, he would run, real slow, with that funny lope, but then he'd stop and make some crack. He was always in command, he knew what he was doing."

In Friz Freleng's *Slick Hare*, waiter Fudd chases Bugs Bunny around the restaurant because Mr. Bogart wants fried rabbit for dinner. Bugs' initial response: "If he wants me, all he has to do is whistle."

Humphrey Bogart was Warner Bros.' biggest star in the 1940s. His tough-guy persona and famous movie roles were often parodied in Looney Tunes cartoons. Bugs got a chance to step into Bogie's shoes, playing the "Rick" role in the Looney Tune epic *Carrotblanca*.

Story meeting
When the story sketches were completed, they were pinned to a large board, and this became the blueprint for the animated cartoon. The entire staff—directors and animators from every unit—were invited to pitch additional gags in a jam session called the "Yes Session." This was named for the fact that no one could say "no" to any idea. After this meeting, the dialog was typed up and recorded.

Richard Wagner
In the early 20th century, Richard Wagner (1813-1883) was the most famous operatic composer in America. He is celebrated for his "music dramas"—operas in which he aimed to perfectly fuse words, music, and stagecraft. This approach is seen in his famous series of operas based on German myths, *The Ring* (*The Rhinegold*, *The Valkyrie*, *Siegfried*, and *Twilight of the Gods*). The characters in *What's Opera, Doc?* are parodies of those from *The Ring*: the hero Siegfried and the woman he loves, the goddess-turned mortal Brunhilde.

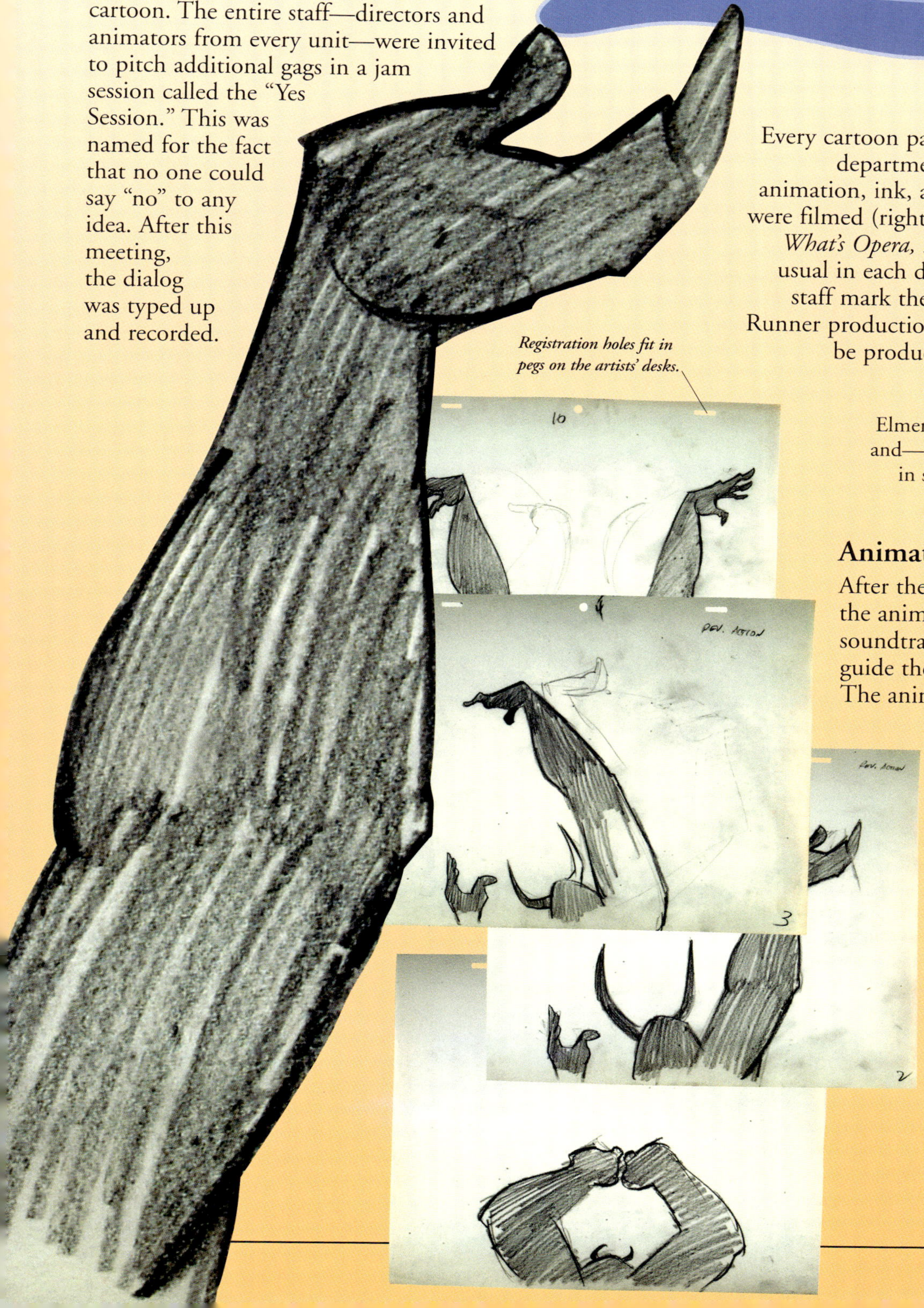

Registration holes fit in pegs on the artists' desks.

Making time
Every cartoon passed through a number of departments—layout, background, animation, ink, and paint—before the cels were filmed (right). The unusually complex *What's Opera, Doc?* required longer than usual in each department. Jones had the staff mark the additional time to Road Runner productions, which he knew could be produced on shorter schedules!

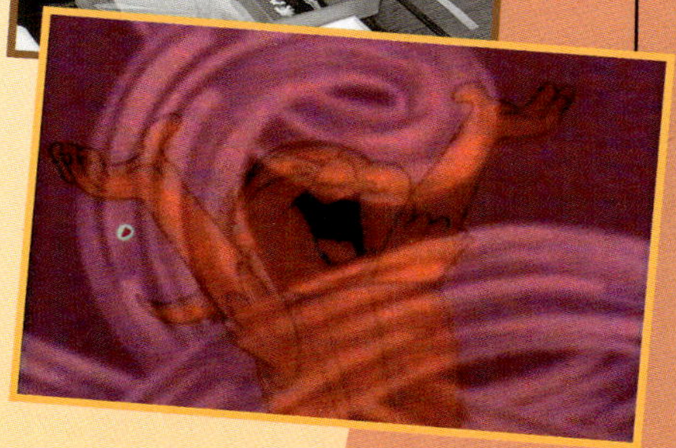

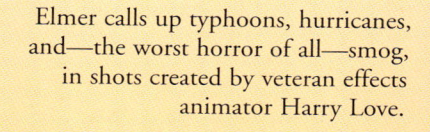

Elmer calls up typhoons, hurricanes, and—the worst horror of all—smog, in shots created by veteran effects animator Harry Love.

Animation drawings
After the voices were recorded, the animators used the timed soundtrack (written on a chart called an "exposure sheet") to guide them as to the number of drawings required in each scene. The animators looked at Jones' layout drawings—and the action indicated on the storyboards—to make the pictures that made the characters appear to move. For each second of film, they drew between 12 and 24 pencil animation drawings.

Magic helmet, Wagnerian demigod-style!

What's Opera Doc? used the vocal talents of Mel Blanc as Bugs and Arthur Q. Bryan as Elmer. On the original vocal track, Bryan yelled the line "Smog!", but Blanc, who could yell like no one else, rerecorded that one word for Elmer.

119

CREATING THE LOOK

THE ART DIRECTOR devises the visual style of a cartoon in collaboration with the director, layout artists, background painters, and animators. Maurice Noble's layouts for *What's Opera, Doc?* employ distorted, expressionist backgrounds and unnaturalistic colors to create a truly breathtaking look. Noble began his career at the Walt Disney studio, where he worked on *Snow White* and *Dumbo*. When he joined Warner Bros., Chuck Jones encouraged him to let his imagination run wild.

Backgrounds were created with gouache paint on board.

Inspired design

Maurice Noble created highly distinctive designs for each film he worked on, often using strong, simple shapes to define the areas where the animation would to take place. For *What's Opera, Doc?*, he produced inspirational color sketches to previsualize the mock operatic setting. "A lot of the story had to be told in graphics," said Jones. "The imagination of the environment was important."

Maurice Noble works on designs at his drawing table.

What's Opera, Doc? contains 104 cuts, a record number for a Merrie Melodies cartoon.

Bugs' obese horse is the Looney Tunes version of Brunhilde's trusty steed, Grane.

One of 500 key animation drawings made by Chuck Jones

Jones and his animation team studied the famed Ballet Russe de Monte Carlo to ensure that the ballet moves in the cartoon were accurate. Every animator put some of their personality into each drawing and movement.

An original pencil drawing by Chuck Jones

Background art
Noble's layouts and De Guard's paintings are dynamic and theatrical, providing a serious backdrop for the absurdity of the Elmer-Bugs chase. "They thought I was bats when I put that bright red on Elmer with those purple skies," said Maurice Noble. "I had the ink and paint department come in and say, 'You really mean you want that magenta red on that?' Yet they thought it was great when they finally saw it on the screen."

Animator Ken Harris brought the Bugs and Elmer ballet to life.

Milt Franklyn's handwritten notes of musical ideas

The foreground foliage is on a separate sheet of clear acetate.

Personal tribute
Chuck Jones said of Maurice Noble, "He never showed off, but he showed up every other layout man I have ever known by his honesty, his devotion to his craft, and, above all, his devotion to the film at hand, and this is nowhere more vividly demonstrated than in *What's Opera, Doc?*"

The musical score
Jones and musical director Milt Franklyn underscored the cartoon with sections of Wagner's operas. "Kill The Wabbit," for example, was adapted from "Ride Of The Valkyries." With cartoons, the dialog is usually recorded in advance of the animation and the music is added afterward. But in the case of *What's Opera, Doc?*, Jones wanted the characters to move in unison with the music, so he recorded the entire music soundtrack first.

The film's grandiose title card

Grand opening
Only a few Looney Tunes cartoons received official premieres; most just opened at downtown theaters without any fanfare. But *What's Opera, Doc?* premiered at the prestigious theater on the Warner Bros. studio lot.

ANIMATED STARS

POKING FUN AT Hollywood was a Looney Tunes tradition. Without doubt, the animators were inspired by screen comedians such as Charlie Chaplin, Buster Keaton, and W.C. Fields. But their close proximity to then-contemporary film stars, by virtue of being on Warner Bros. main lot, gave the cartoonists the opportunity to lampoon the personalities, visual characteristics, and famous roles of Hollywood's greatest.

Smoldering star
In Bob Clampett's *Bacall To Arms*, a wolf goes to the movies and dozes right through—until Laurie Becool (a cartoon version of Lauren Bacall) appears and drives him wild with her sexy stare.

Bugs Marx the spot
Bugs Bunny has been compared to all three of the subversive Marx Brothers—Groucho in particular. Bugs' line, "Of course you know, this means war!", was originally spoken by Groucho in the 1933 Marx Brothers movie *Duck Soup*. The wabbit himself donned a Groucho disguise in *Slick Hare* and *Wideo Wabbit*.

Just like Groucho's, Bugs' eyebrows are painted on.

Bugs usually has good dress sense, but in this case he's made an exception.

Bugs with Groucho trademark mustache and cigar... er, carrot

Frankly my dear...
Clark Gable was the king of Hollywood leading men. Vocal mimic Kent Rogers parodied Gable's voice in Avery's *Hollywood Steps Out*, where the movie hunk is chasing a blonde—who in the end turns out to be Groucho in drag! Ouch!

Groucho club
Tex Avery compared Bugs Bunny to the cigar-chomping, fast-talking Marx brother: "You should visualize him as Groucho Marx. If he ever runs from anyone, he has a trick in mind. If you look back at the old Grouchos, he would run, real slow, with that funny lope, but then he'd stop and make some crack. He was always in command, he knew what he was doing."

In Friz Freleng's *Slick Hare*, waiter Fudd chases Bugs Bunny around the restaurant because Mr. Bogart wants fried rabbit for dinner. Bugs' initial response: "If he wants me, all he has to do is whistle."

Humphrey Bogart was Warner Bros.' biggest star in the 1940s. His tough-guy persona and famous movie roles were often parodied in Looney Tunes cartoons. Bugs got a chance to step into Bogie's shoes, playing the "Rick" role in the Looney Tune epic *Carrotblanca*.

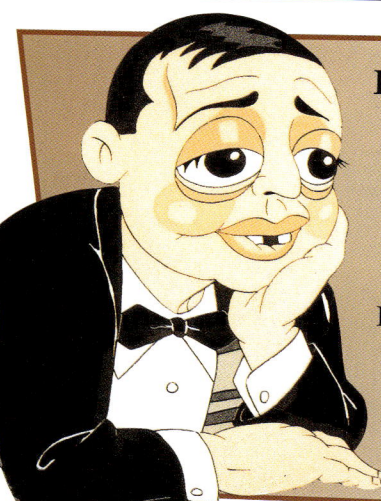

Lots of Lorre
The Hungarian-born movie actor Peter Lorre, with his gap-toothed smile and bulging eyes, often played mysterious or psychotic characters. The Looney Tunes frequently caricatured him, using the vocal talents of Kent Rogers. Tweety does a take-off in *Carrotblanca*, and he was cast as mad scientists in *Birth Of A Notion* and *Hare-Raising Hare* (above).

Tweety does his Peter Lorre impression.

Jack Benny
Mel Blanc was a regular performer on Jack Benny's satirical radio program and the Warner Bros. animators were all fans. In turn, Benny appears in several cartoons, notably in *Malibu Beach Party*.

Porky Pig disguises himself as slapstick comedian Oliver Hardy to sneak onto the Warner Bros. movie lot in You Ought To Be In Pictures.

'Tec meets 'tec
The appearance of England's most famous detective, Sherlock Holmes, gives Daffy as Duck Twacy quite a surprise in *The Great Piggy Bank Robbery*. The duck recovers enough to deliver a put-down: "Scram Sherlock! I'm workin' this side of the street!" Daffy later got a chance to mispronounce Cockney slang when he portrayed the super-sleuth himself in Chuck Jones' *Deduce You Say*, as "Dorlock Homes," with Porky as "Watkins."

Daffy demands movie executives' time in Looney Tunes: Back In Action.

My little chickadee
Though best remembered as a verbal comedian, W.C. Fields had a unique visual presence which was often caricatured. Seen here as a pig having dinner with a Katherine Hepburn-esque horse in *Coo-Coo Nut Grove*, the Fields persona also starred in *Cracked Ice* and *Shop, Look, and Listen* (as a loud mouthed mouse).

The Looney Tunes version of W.C. Fields

Back In Action
Brendan Fraser, Steve Martin, Bill Murray, Michael Jordan—today's biggest stars are lining up to work with Looney Tunes. The Warner Bros. creations are recognized as Hollywood legends: they have won five Oscars, Bugs has a star on the Hollywood Walk of Fame, and the characters have been honored on U.S. postage stamps.

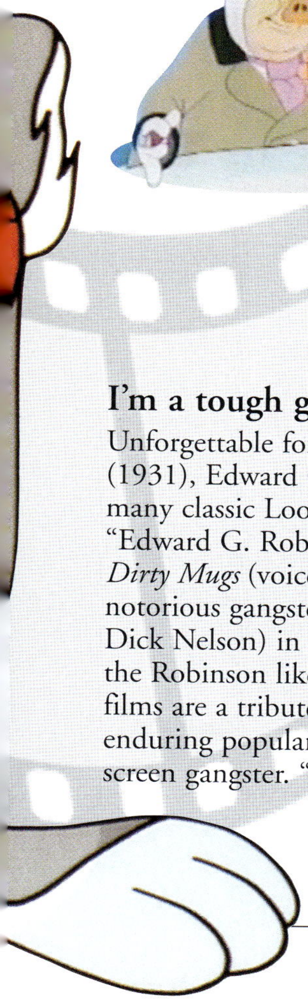

I'm a tough guy, see!
Unforgettable for playing tough-guy Rico in *Little Caeser* (1931), Edward G. Robinson has been caricatured in many classic Looney Tunes. From the killer-diller dog "Edward G. Robbersome" in Tex Avery's *Thugs With Dirty Mugs* (voiced by Danny Webb) to the notorious gangster Rocky (voiced by Dick Nelson) in *Racketeer Rabbit*, the Robinson likeness in these films are a tribute to the enduring popularity of this screen gangster. "See?"

Rabbit ears, see?

The fat man
Bugs Bunny runs into this caracature of rotund actor Sidney Greenstreet in *Slick Hare*. Greenstreet was a villain in many Warner Bros. movies, including the Humphrey Bogart classics *The Maltese Falcon*, *Across The Pacific*, and *Casablanca*.

THE GOOD FIGHT

BUGS, DAFFY, PORKY, and the other Looney Tunes spend much of their time fighting each other, so it's no surprise that they've been drafted into the armed forces at times. Warner Bros. cartoons that showed the military life were an opportunity to cast the Looney Tunes in a patriotic light, fighting for America and putting down tyranny. In addition, certain new characters were created to educate and train the troups.

Private Snafu

The Private Snafu cartoons, aimed at the servicemen and women of the U.S. Army, showed what *not* to do to stay alive. Many of the films were written by Theodore Geisel (a.k.a. Dr. Seuss) and produced by the Warner Bros. cartoon staff.

Private Snafu cartoons were directed by Chuck Jones, Friz Freleng, Frank Tashlin, and Bob Clampett. Mel Blanc provided voices and Carl Stalling supervised the music. In keeping with their military settings, the films included many jokes and situations based on the lives of soldiers.

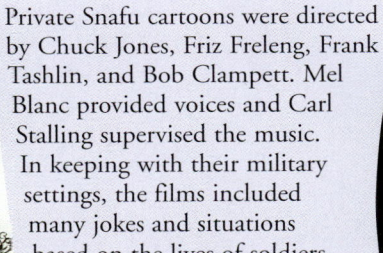

Seaman Hook

Warner Bros. produced cartoons for the U.S. Navy featuring Seaman Hook, a sailor who constantly looked forward to a happy future as a civilian. Hank Ketchum (who created the comic-strip character, Dennis The Menace) devised Hook, and the films were variously directed by Chuck Jones, Robert McKimson, and Bob Clampett.

Snafu's name is an acronym of a popular Army complaint—Situation Normal: All Fouled Up.

Technical Fairy First Class is a rough-tough army sprite who comes to Snafu's aid on various occasions—on one occasion turning him into a "Snafuperman"!

Model sheet showing Technical Fairy First Class

To demonstrate the correct course of action, Pvt. Snafu did everything wrong.

This original pencil animation, from Operation Snafu, shows Snafu running from the enemy—again!

Uncle Sam

The famous character of Uncle Sam in his striped pants personifies the United States of America. The spirit of Uncle Sam visits Porky Pig in *Old Glory*, directed by Chuck Jones, and teaches him the meaning of the Pledge Of Allegiance. The film recreates famous moments in American history through dramatic, realistic character animation that is unlike any ever seen before in Warner Bros. cartoons.

The drill sergeant is no match for Bugs Bunny.

In Chuck Jones' *Forward March Hare*, Bugs Bunny is mistaken for a man and put through boot camp training—until his big feet and long ears give him away.

Life on the homefront

Some Looney Tunes spoofed wartime life on the home front. *Wacky Blackout* (left) showed the effects of food rationing on animals and insects, while *Scrap Happy Daffy* has patriotic Daffy Duck collecting scrap metal for victory.

Comic books

The Looney Tunes not only boosted wartime morale on screen, but did likewise in print. Bugs and Porky urged readers to buy war bonds and stamps to help win the war effort—and comics like these became scarce as they were collected for recycling or sent to soldiers overseas. Because the Looney Tunes were street-smart contemporary characters, their attitudes perfectly reflected the patriotic mood of the American public during times of threat.

The three big guns, Bugs Bunny, Porky Pig, and Elmer Fudd, rally for the cause.

Porky scolds some mountain men for feuding among themselves while the world is at war against a true threat, in a scene from *Looney Tunes Comic #10*.

As everyone knows, gremlins are little pests who wreck military aircraft with "dia-bolical saba-togee." In *Falling Hare*, Bugs spots one of them laying into a plane with a mallet, which leads to a midair battle of wills between hare and sprite.

Ralph Phillips, the little boy in *From A To Z-Z-Z-Z*, grows up and features in a pair of Army recruitment films produced by Warner Bros. Animation.

Ralph joins the Volunteer Army in Drafty Isn't It.

Pete and Re-Pete convince Ralph to reenlist.

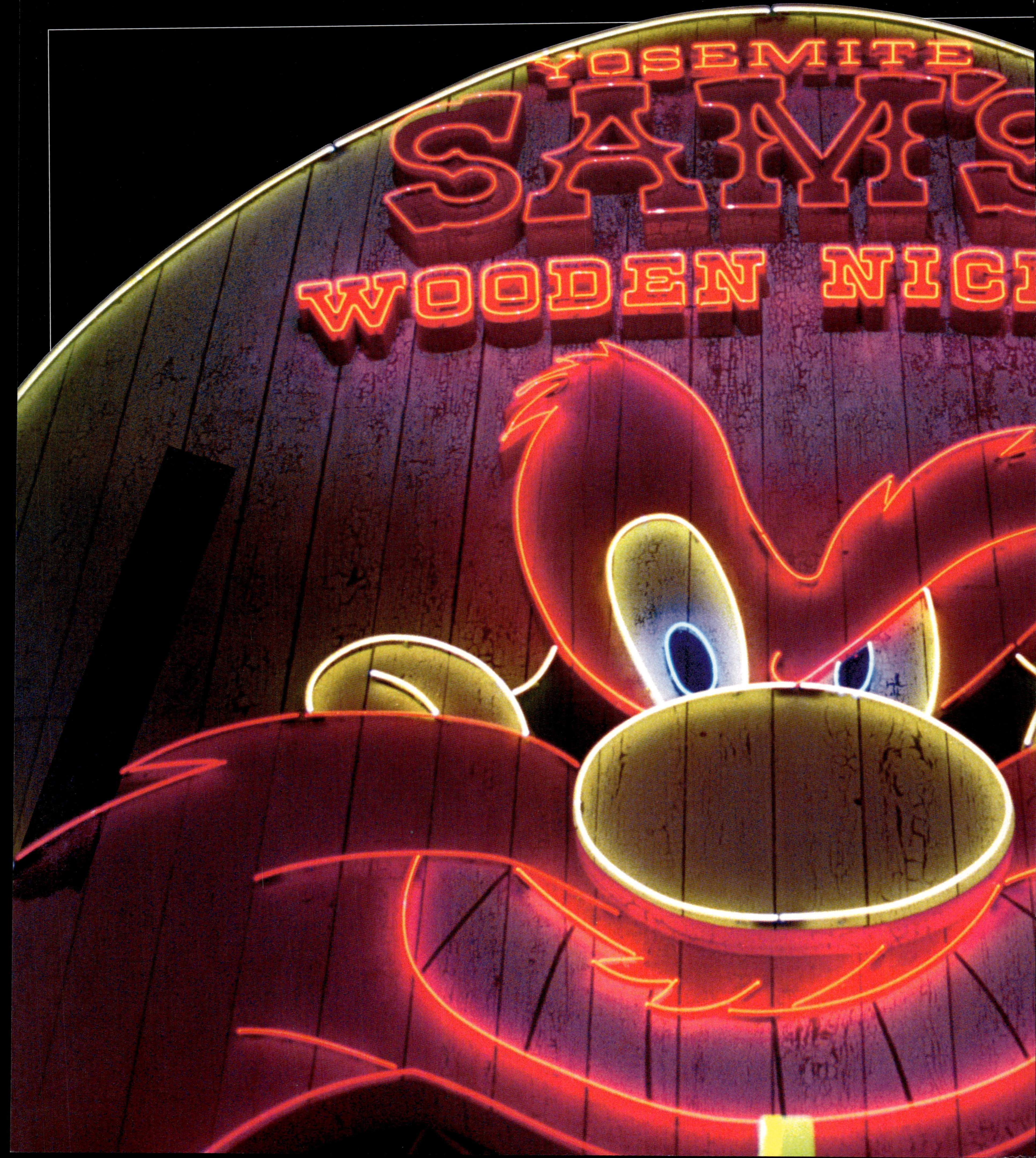
YOSEMITE
SAM'S
WOODEN

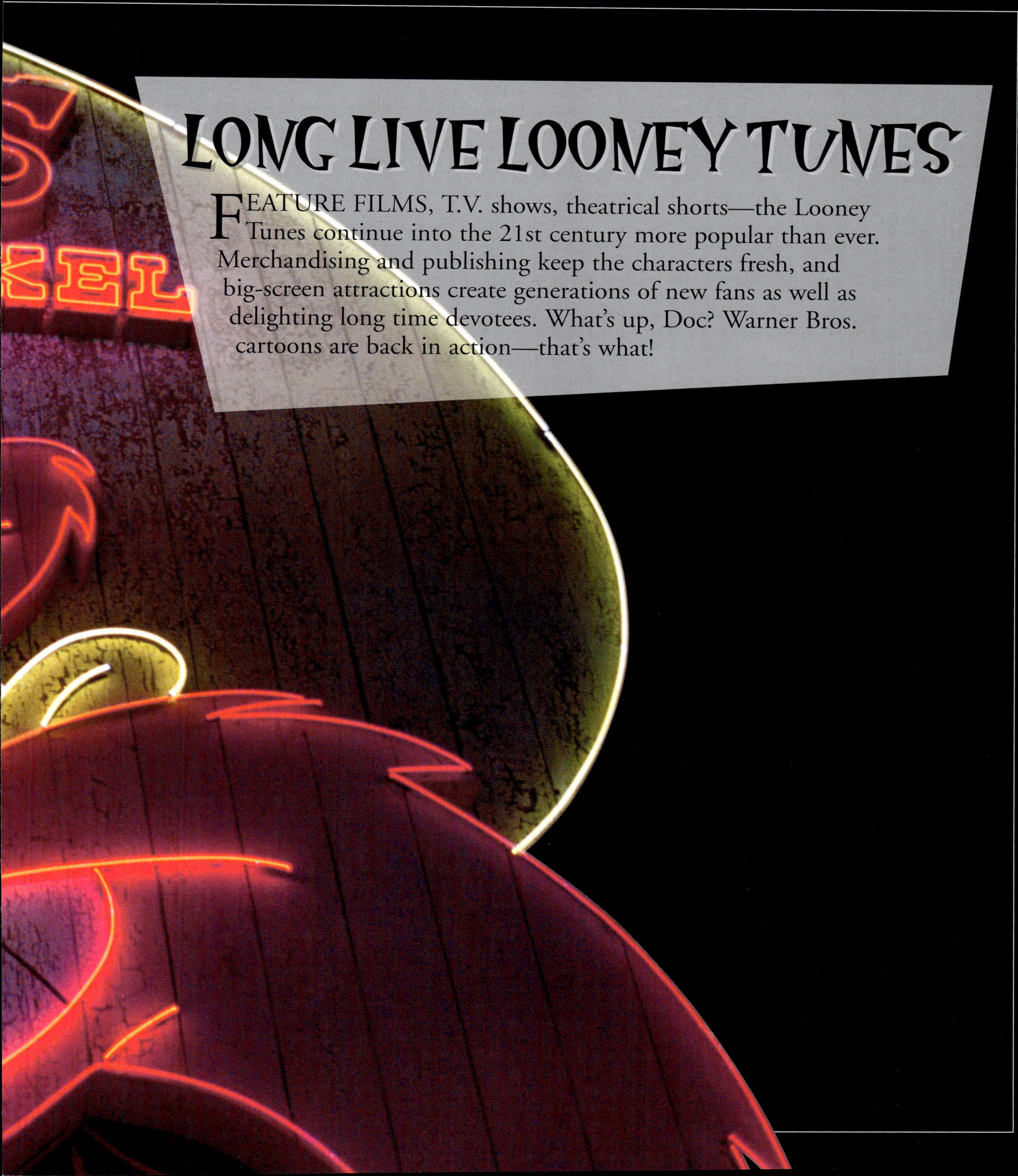

LONG LIVE LOONEY TUNES

FEATURE FILMS, T.V. shows, theatrical shorts—the Looney Tunes continue into the 21st century more popular than ever. Merchandising and publishing keep the characters fresh, and big-screen attractions create generations of new fans as well as delighting long time devotees. What's up, Doc? Warner Bros. cartoons are back in action—that's what!

MERCHANDISE

FOLLOWING HIS MANY YEARS producing cartoons for Warner Bros., Leon Schlesinger continued to play a vital role at the company when he became its first merchandising executive. Although the Looney Tunes cartoons appealed to all age groups, manufacturers have traditionally aimed licensed products at children. Most of the items pictured here were manufactured during the golden age of animation, while the original classic cartoons were still in production.

R. Dakin and Co. made the first vinyl Elmer Fudd doll.

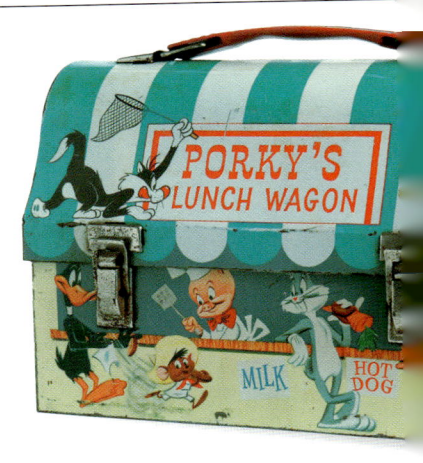

A metal lunch box, issued by Thermos Products, features a range of characters, including Bugs eating a carrot burger!

Cine film

In the days before home video, cartoons were released on 8mm film for home projection. Many Looney Tunes and Merrie Melodies were released in black and white, silent, edited formats—but toon fans and aspiring animators were grateful to rescreen these classic movie moments.

Papa Bear from The Three Bears cartoons

Umbrella rotates when key is turned

Tin Porky

Porky's popularity rivaled that of Mickey Mouse and Popeye during the Depression era. U.S. toy company Marx made some of the first wind-up tin toys of the Looney Tunes star.

Bugs and Porky have been sending warm wishes on greeting cards for more than 50 years.

A "Merrie" Christmas tree ornament

Bugs speaks!

This 24-inch (61-cm) tall pull-string "Talking Bugs Bunny" stuffed doll, with vinyl face and hands, featured Mel Blanc asking, "What's up, doc?" and seven other phrases. It was first released by Mattel during the premiere of the ABC-TV network Bugs Bunny Show. Talking hand puppets of Bugs and Porky were also released.

Sylvester and Tweety toys were aimed at younger tots.

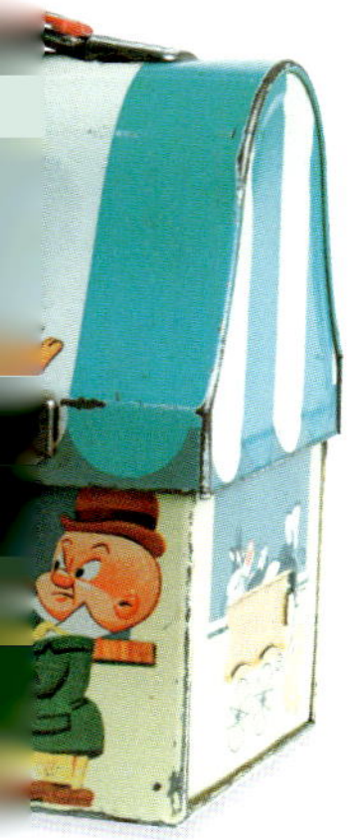

Popular pigs

Ceramic figures of Porky and Petunia have become some of the rarest collectibles. The prominence of Porky and Petunia on merchandise, even when Bugs, Daffy, and others eclipsed them on the screen, was due to their popularity as comic-book stars. Porky not only had his own book, but regularly featured as Bugs' sidekick in the earliest years of the strips.

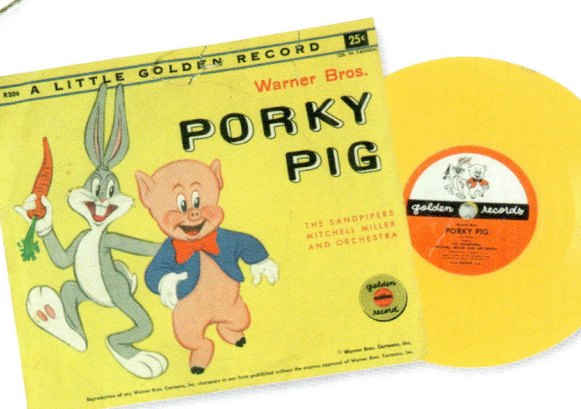

Little Golden Records often feature Mitch Miller's orchestra singing a forgettable tune. Today, they are beloved by the baby boomers who cherished them as children.

Bugs Bunny toys

Bugs has been known to rattle Elmer Fudd and Yosemite Sam—but here is the real thing (left)! Mattel created many toys, including a Bugs Bunny wind-up guitar (below left). The artwork on Mattel's pop-up music box (below), like much vintage merchandise, was created by the artists at the cartoon studio. The "Bugs Bunny And His Pals" flashlites and finger animation cards (above) allowed children to put on their own puppet shows.

Eyes move when key turned.

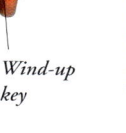

Sam figure

The metal pistols and cloth whiskers of this Yosemite Sam doll (made by R. Dakin and Co.) fall off easily, making the complete item a hotly sought-after collectible.

Wind-up key

Original packaging

Money-bank Beaky

Among the most popular Looney Tunes collectibles from the golden age are the desktop items made by the Moss Metal Co. These money banks, pencil holders, and bookends featured Bugs Bunny, Porky Pig, Elmer Fudd, Daffy Duck, Sniffles the Mouse, and Beaky Buzzard (left, standing beside a bank in the shape of a tree trunk).

And beyond...

Looney Tunes are still widely merchandized today on such products as mouse pads, cell phones, electric tooth brushes, and food packaging. This telephone is adorned with hungry Sylvester and Tweety (who hides inside the garbage pail).

Look out for Tweety!

PUBLISHING

COMIC BOOKS, coloring books, storybooks of all shapes and sizes—The Looney Tunes in print have become cherished children's reading and hot collectors items. The artwork and stories for these publications were often created by the actual artists and writers behind the original cartoons: such luminaries as Tom McKimson, Pete Alvarado, Michael Maltese, and Tedd Pierce.

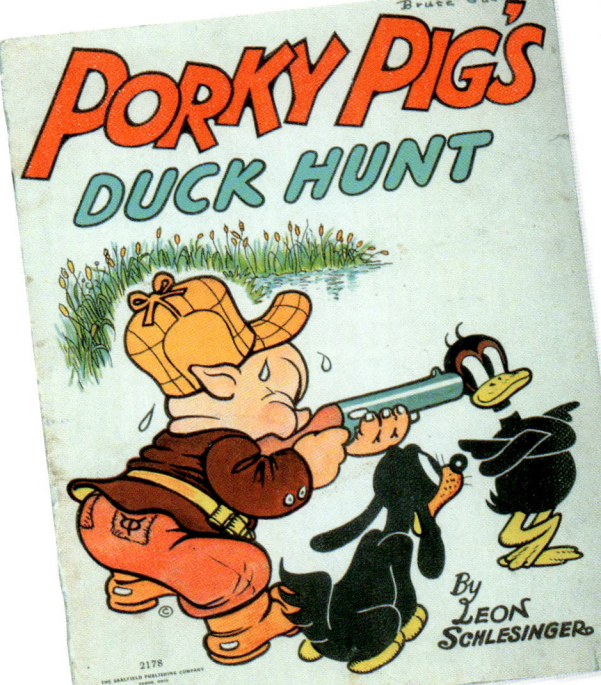

Earliest book
Based on Tex Avery's *Porky's Duck Hunt*, which starred a new screwball character named Daffy Duck, this book is one of the earliest-known Looney Tunes print tie-ins. As with many early storybooks, producer Leon Schlesinger is credited on the jacket for the story and art.

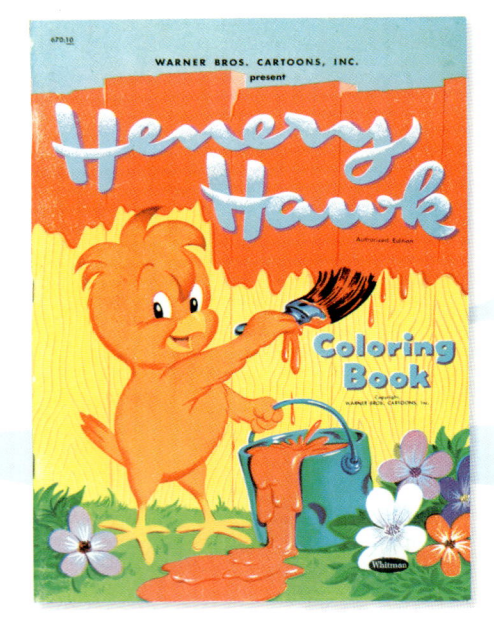

Between the lines
Coloring books were so popular that co-stars such as Henerey Hawk and Elmer Fudd got a chance to highlight their own books!

Big Little Books
Western Publishing Co. created picture storybooks in all shapes and sizes. Big Little Books and Better Little Books were chunky books that were small enough to fit into little readers' hands.

Big value
When Western first began publishing Big Little Books and other formats, they were originally sold for 10 cents. Most were between 240 and 320 pages long!

Wile E. Coyote reads ACME catalogs to order Road Runner-catching devices.

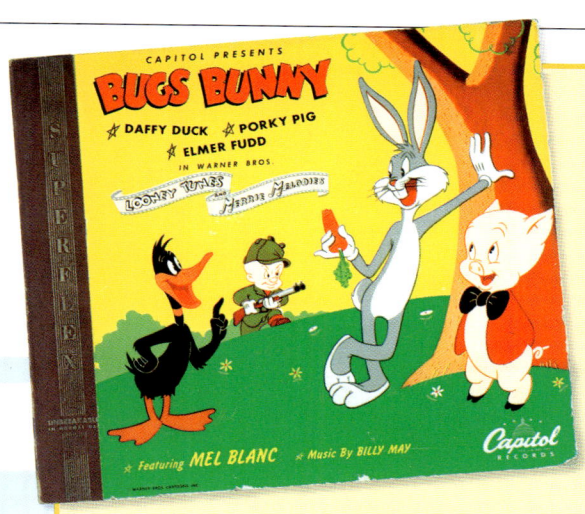

Bugs Bunny (above) featured three stories: "Bugs Bunny Meets Elmer Fudd," "Porky Pig In Africa," and "Daffy Duck Flies South."

"Talking" books
Capitol Records contracted with Mel Blanc to appear in an audio series originally sold as 78 rpm vinyl records. The albums were accompanied by story books illustrated by either Robert, Tom, or Charles McKimson.

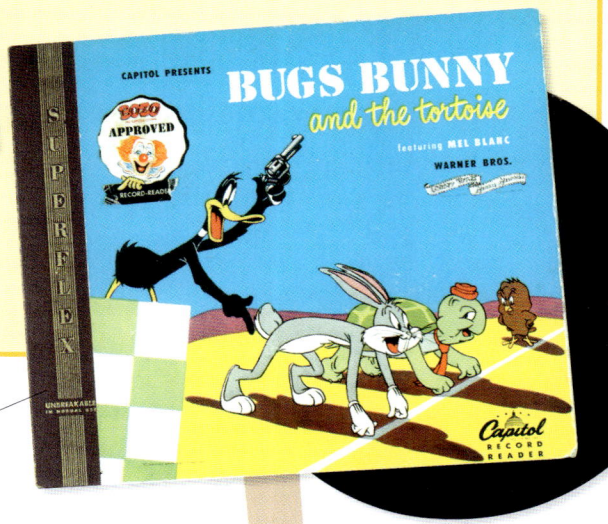

The story features Cecil Tortoise from Tortoise Beats Hare.

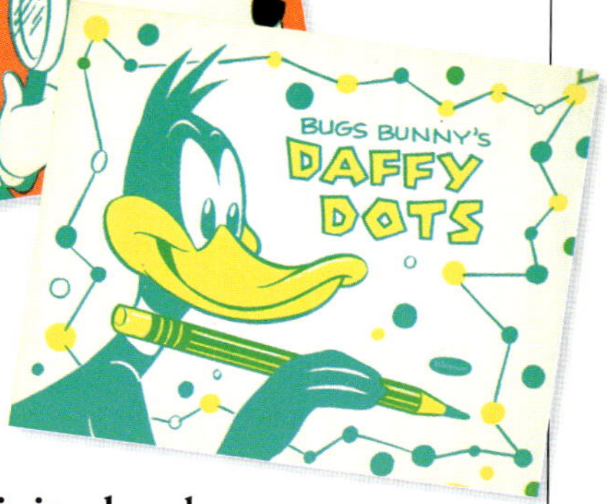

Activity books
Cutout books, sticker albums, connect-the-dots, paper dolls, and other activity books are a staple at drug and toy stores. These two were published by Whitman, a subsidiary of Western Publishing Co.

Premiums and giveaways
Special publications were created for promotional purposes. Looney Tunes character comics were included in packages of Cheerios cereal, Quaker Oats Puffed Rice, and Kool Aid. Special issues of March Of Comics featuring Bugs or Porky were distributed at Sears department stores.

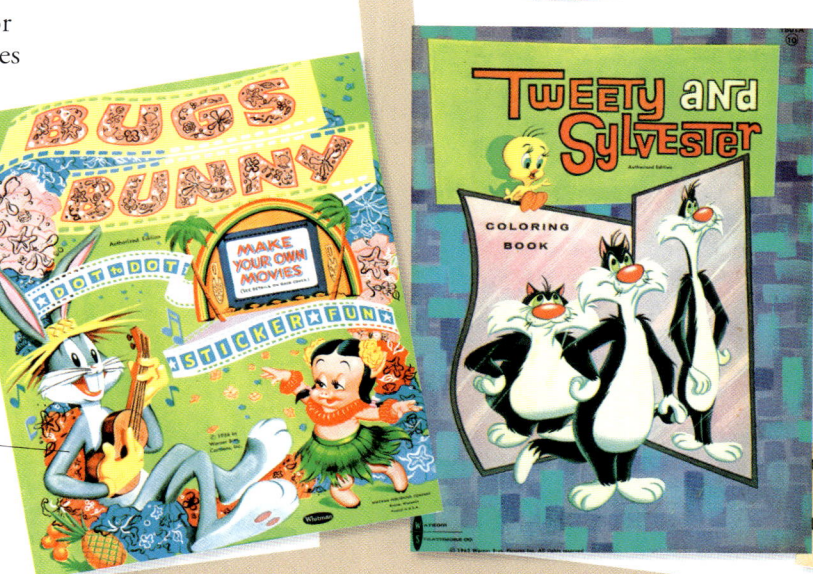

Books and comics often feature Looney Tunes characters in very different guises to the cartoon films.

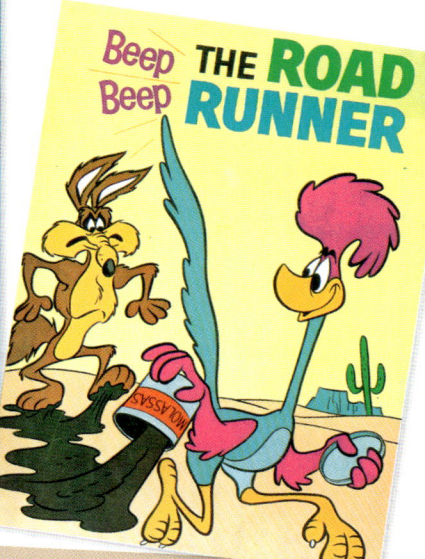

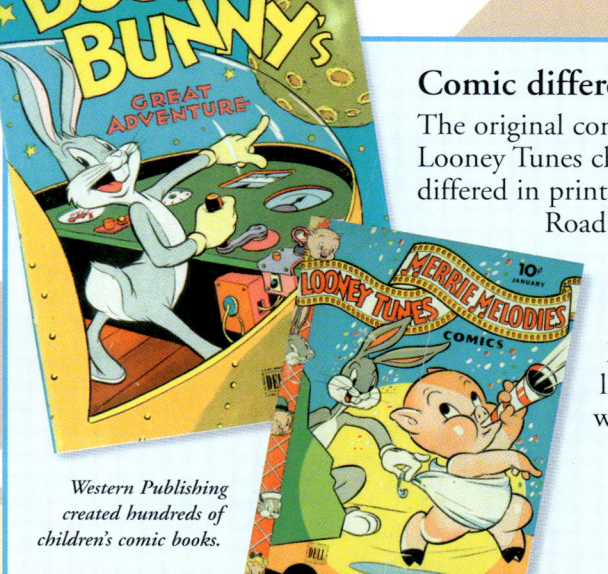

Comic differences
The original comic-book personas for the Looney Tunes characters sometimes differed in print from the animated films. Road Runner, for example, spoke and ran through the desert with his three nephews in the comics, while Sniffles the Mouse was teamed with a little girl named Mary Jane, who had magic powers.

Western Publishing created hundreds of children's comic books.

War Bonds provided extra revenue for the war effort.

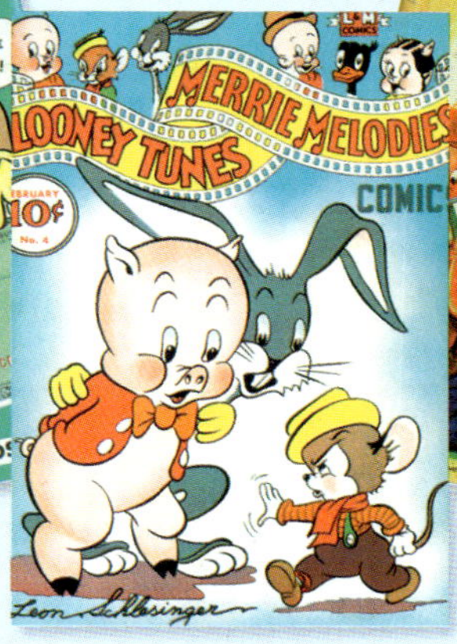

BACK IN ACTION 1

IN THEIR BIGGEST feature film yet, Bugs Bunny and Daffy Duck co-star with actors Brendan Fraser, Jenna Elfman, and Steve Martin in *Looney Tunes: Back In Action*. Blockbuster action combines with spectacular animation and a hilarious story which, like the classic shorts, breaks the fourth wall and runs off in surprising directions—all strictly for laughs!

The plot

When Daffy Duck and security guard D.J. Drake (Fraser) are fired from Warner Bros., Bugs Bunny and Vice President of Comedy Kate (Elfman) follow them. The four set off to rescue Drake's missing father—action star Damian Drake (Timothy Dalton), who is really a spy being hunted by the chairman of the Acme Corporation (Martin).

The story starts on the actual Warner Bros. backlot in Burbank, California.

Damian's Drake's rocket-powered spy car is filled with cool gadgets.

An all-star cast

Timothy Dalton, Heather Locklear, pro-wrestler Bill Goldberg, and NASCAR's champion racer Jeff Gordon provide co-starring roles and cameo appearances. Looney Tunes appearing in the film include Tweety, Wile E. Coyote, Marvin The Martian, Granny, and many others.

Joe Dante

Director Joe Dante directed *Gremlins*, *Small Soldiers*, and *The Howling*, but the Looney Tunes proved his greatest challenge. Bugs was the hardest of all: "Because of his persona, the fact that he has to remain cool at all times and always be on top of everything," Dante recalls. "Daffy is much more malleable because he's crazy and has neuroses."

The movie includes scenes inside Yosemite Sam's casino.

Watch out for in-jokes in the casino, including a photo of Chuck Jones!

Eric Goldberg

Animation Supervisor Eric Goldberg is a veteran Disney animator who co-directed the features *Pocahontas* and *Fantasia 2000* and created the animation of the genie in *Aladdin*. His career has been influenced by his personal friendships with Looney Tunes luminaries Chuck Jones, animator Ken Harris, and layout artist Maurice Noble.

Bugs and Daffy

Eric Goldberg thinks Bugs is the greatest animation character ever, but he admits that this is Daffy's movie. "He steals every scene he's in," says Goldberg. "And after all those years of being a second banana, I think he deserves it!"

The movie stays true to the classic personas of the Looney Tunes.

BACK IN ACTION 2

TO MAKE THE MOVIE, a new world had to be created—a place where cartoons and people "don't discriminate against each other, don't act surprised when a talking duck walks into a room," as director Joe Dante explains. Of course, the world of *Looney Tunes: Back In Action* also had to be designed and built by talented craftsmen at Warner Bros. in Hollywood.

Acme headquarters

The power-hungry Acme Corporation is the setting where Mr. Chairman (Steve Martin) plots to rule the world—once he can snatch the fabled Blue Monkey diamond from Daffy, Bugs, and D.J. Drake. "Steve Martin ad libbed 90 percent of his part and created a character that wasn't in the script," says director Dante. "Steve made him a wonderfully crazy Looney Tune kind of a guy."

The Acme chairman plans to use the diamond's power to superevolve the company, giving it "an unbeatable edge in a tight marketplace"!

Paris

One of the most memorable animation sequences in the film is Bugs', Daffy's, and Elmer's chase through the Louvre art museum in Paris. They jump in and out of various famous paintings and take on the style of each one, melting in the Dali and becoming pointillist in the Seurat.

A preproduction drawing depicts Paris.

Los Angeles Exposition Park stood in for Paris in some scenes.

Production designer Bill Brzeski gave Acme's monolithic headquarters a retro-futuristic look.

When in France, do as Pepe Le Pew does.

Getting the lines right

The movie called for vocal specialists who could match the voices of the characters we all know—and Mel Blanc is a hard act to follow! "There's no one alive who can do that many different voices," says director Joe Dante. Joe Alasky voiced Daffy and Bugs in this feature, after years of providing such stellar performances as Yosemite Sam and Sylvester.

Elaborate jungle locations were created on soundstages in Burbank.

Pre-production artists visualized the settings months before filming began.

Special techniques

Computer effects were utilized in a final space chase sequence and for some of the props the cartoon characters handle. A new computer process called Lumo was also used to "light" the two dimensional characters, giving them a realistic sense of depth.

Blueprint of jungle set

Animation

The traditional 2D animation was produced out of Warner Bros. Animation studios in Sherman Oaks, California. The studio houses a 500 member animation team—from layout, effects, and digital artists to character animators, painters and compositors.

Blue Monkey

"If the bad guys get the diamond, they'll plunge the earth into an endless night of evil!" explains D.J. Everyone is after fabled Blue Monkey diamond—of course, Daffy only wants it to satisfy his own greedy desires.

The Blue Money diamond is actually red!

"I'm rich! I'm affluent! My liquidity is assured!"

135

TO THE FUTURE

THE CLASSIC WARNER BROS. CARTOONS are considered timeless, but the Looney world moves on. As long as the future continues to offer fresh opportunities for adventure, the Looney Tunes characters will be there, zany as ever. Daffy Duck's famous role as retro space-hero Duck Dodgers (in the 24½th century) has been expanded into a TV series that takes him into intergalactic battle against a universe of Merrie Martians. "Space will never be the same!"

Dr. I.Q. Hi is the Secretary of the Stratosphere. His inventions include the Frost Pen, the Flatulence Pill, and the Holographic Collar.

Duck Dodgers

Defrosted after 351 years, Daffy Duck convinces the Earth's Defensive Protectorate that he is a hero from the 21st century (he lied on his resume). He is given a ship called the *Sisyphus* and a crew: namely the Eager Young Space Cadet, Porky Pig. Together they form a galactic force that must stand up against Earth's major foe: Mars, and its Martian Commander X-2 (played by Marvin the Martian).

K-9 is very adept a retrieving dynamite sticks.

With the aid of a rare mineral called Moonesium, our Space Cadet becomes Pork Piggler, Pig of Action!

Form-fitting uniform can withstand ray gun blasts at 20 paces!

Old foes

Marvin the Martian (or Commander X-2, as he prefers to be called) is willing to do absolutely anything for his Martian Queen (whom he is sweet on). With the aid of his loyal canine assistant K-9 and a ready supply of Instant Martians, X-2 challenges Duck Dodgers on lost planet golf courses, in intergalactic casinos, and along deep-space drag races.

Commander X-2 a.k.a. Marvin, Buckethead, or "Spitoonikus"

Martian fleet

Commander X-2's starship is called the *Triumph*. Through his diligence, Marvin has kept the ship in excellent shape. When not in battle, the crew can enjoy an oil bath, eat at the feastatorium, or watch a robo-gladiator battle in the arena.

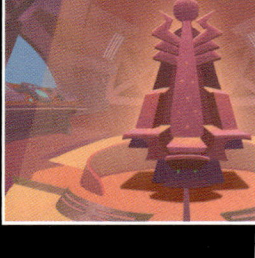

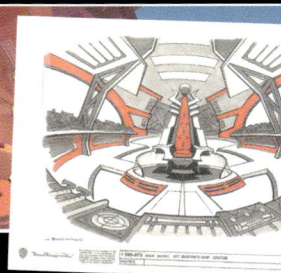

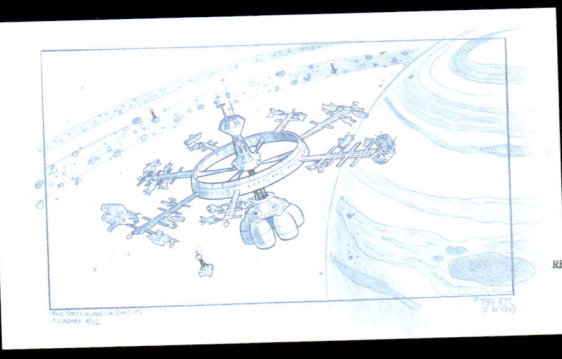

Space port

A layout sketch illustrates the attention to detail the new Duck Dodgers series enjoys courtesy of animation directors Spike Brandt and Tony Cervone (who developed the series with writer/producer Paul Dini). Both artists worked on the feature film *Space Jam* and the theatrical shorts *Little Go Beep* and *Carrotblanca*.

Mission to Mars

Marvin the Martian and the fearless Duck Dodgers are showcased on the Space Squadron patches for two NASA Mars Exploration Rover Missions launched in 2003. The special patches were worn by Team Delta crews, comprising members from NASA, the United States Air Force, and Boeing. Additionally, these emblems appear in the mission control booth and at the Air Force launch pad.

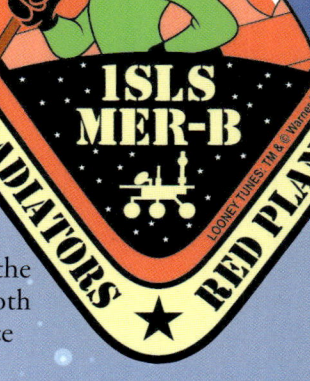

The better to hear you with.

The better to hit you with.

General S'am

General Krutchat-kuh S'am, a nasty barbarian with a long, red mustache (and an uncanny resemblance to a certain earthbound varmint) is the leader of the Klunkin warriors, who have their sights set on conquering Earth. Dodgers and his Space Cadet have been warned to stay away, but that doesn't stop them. Crash-landing on their home world, Pig and Duck defeat the danger and save the universe!

Earth's Defensive Protectorate is the headquarters for Duck Dodgers, space-hero Star Johnson, Dr. I.Q. Hi, and various eager young space cadets.

"With great power, comes a permissible degree of power abuse!"

Green Lantern

After a mix up at the dry cleaners, Duck Dodgers dons a Green Lantern costume and power ring. Luckily, Dodgers uses his new powers to foil space villain Sinestro and duly receives eternal thanks—and his original space suit back—from Hal Jordan, the original Green Lantern.

Back on Earth

A series of new Looney Tunes were made for theaters in 2003. Produced by Larry Doyle (*The Simpsons*, *Beavis and Butthead*), they place old favorites in new situations. In *Wizard of Ow*, Wile E. Coyote uses an old magic book (and Acme black magic) to try to catch the Road Runner.

Acme magic broom—goes boom!

Road Runner—still running in a theater near you!

INDEX

More than just an index, this combined index and character guide is a fact-fuelled database on a galaxy of Looney Tune personalities. Use the numbered chart (right) and the book's endpapers to identify the unsung bit-players.

Beans meets a monster in *Hollywood Capers*.

Key

Number in brackets refers to character chart (top right) and endpapers.

Numbers indicate pages on which character appears in the book.

Bugs Bunny (**1**) 8-9, 10-11, 12-13, 24, 25, 28

Butch J. Bulldog (**143**) and Puppy (**142**)
When tough Butch sires a son in *Pappy's Puppy*, cat chasing is the first thing the pup must learn.

Characters not appearing elsewhere in the book have a gazetteer entry, explaining who they are.

A
Abominable Snowman (**108**) 21, 29
Academy of Motion Picture Arts and Sciences 117
Acme Corp. 53, 60, 66-67, 68-69, 72, 134
A. Flea (**49**) 104
Agatha and Emily (**7**) 84
Alice *see* Honey-Mousers, the
Allen, Fred 46
Alvarado, Pete 115
animation
 computer-generated 15, 135
 timing for 119
 in relation to music 121
Ant Hill Harry *see* Baby Face Finster
Army recruitment films 125
Avery, Tex 53, 107, 111, 113, 122

B
Babbit and Catstello 56
Baby Face Finster (**195**) 96
Baby Face Half-Nelson 97
Bacall, Lauren 122
background art 114-115
Back In Action see Looney Tunes: Back In Action
Ballet Russe 120
Banty 46
Barnyard Dawg (**112**) 46, 47, 50, 85, 100
Bartholomew (**110**) 89
Batty (**17**) 99, 104
B.B. Wolf (**23**) and Nephew (**26**)
In *The Turn-Tale Wolf*, Nephew Wolf is ashamed of his big, bad uncle having huffed and puffed pigs' houses down. B.B. denies it, retelling the tale so he's the innocent one and the three pigs are the bad guys.

In *The Abominable Snow Rabbit*, a snowman is looking for a bunny named George.

138

Beaky Buzzard (**18**) 18, 84, 129
Beans 32, 98, 114
Bee (**5**)
 In *Porky's Pastry Pirates*, this tough bee teaches his dumb fly friend how to steal food from Porky Pig's bakery. The fly gets swatted, not fed—then borrows Porky's swatter to use on the bee.
Benaderet, Bea 62, 83
Benny 61, 99
Benny, Jack 103, 123
Bernier, Buddy 32
Bertie (**170**) 52, 98, 102, 113
Big Bad Wolf (**148**)
 This loopy lupine doesn't want to eat *The Three Little Bops*—he'd rather play trumpet in their band. When rejected, though, he resorts to typical fairy tale tactics—huffing and puffing and blowing the pigs' nightclubs down.
Big Ghost (**20**) and Little Ghost (**21**)
 In *Ghost Wanted*, Little Ghost applies for haunting lessons at 1313 Dracula Drive—and spends the day being terrorized by Big Ghost's expert scares.
Black Fury 35
Black Widow Spider *see* Moth
Blanc, Mel 14, 32, 34, 40, 43, 46, 57, 80, 90, 102, 103, 112, 113, 118, 119, 123, 124, 128
Blacque Jacque Shellaque (**187**) 13
Bletcher, Billy 83
Bogart, Humphrey 122
books 130-131
Bookworm (**36**) 78
Bosko 106, 107, 114
Boy (**172**) and Girl (**173**) Mouse
 In *Mouse Warming*, Boy Mouse wants Girl Mouse—and Claude Cat wants a Boy Mouse dinner, tricking him with phony love notes from his mate. The mice get even by writing Claude a love note of their own—which they ascribe to Claude's bulldog enemy.
Boyer, Charles 43
Brandt, Spike 134
Brown, Bernard 107, 111
Bruno (Bosko's dog) 106
Bruno the Magnificent (**124**) 95
Bryan, Arthur Q. 14, 36, 118, 119
Brzeski, Bill 134
Buck Rogers 45

Buddy 107, 114
Bull, the (**125**) 21, 90
Bunny (**128**) and Claude (**129**) 89
Bugs Bunny (**1**)
 8-9, 10-11, 12-13, 24, 25, 28, 29, 36, 37, 38, 40, 41, 45, 51, 62, 71, 75, 79, 84, 87, 90, 93, 95, 96, 97, 101, 103, 105, 110, 111, 112, 113, 114, 116, 118, 122, 123, 125, 132, 133, 134, 135
 in drag 18–19
 in war 125
 in toys 128, 129
 his voice 14
Bugs Bunny Road Runner Movie, the 117
Butch J. Bulldog (**143**) and Puppy (**142**)
 When tough Butch sires a son in *Pappy's Puppy*, cat chasing is the first thing the pup must learn. Sylvester is cat enough to beat the little varmint—but Butch makes sure Sylvester takes the beatings.
Butler, Daws 89, 103

A baby elephant turns baseball hero in *Hobo Bobo*.

C
Capitol Records 58, 79
Captain, the cat 99
Captain Video 45
Carmen Miranda 16, 19
Carr, Jack 107
Cartoon Network 45
Casbah (**149**) 51

Sam's fire-sneezing dragon in *Knighty Knight Bugs*

catchphrases 56, 57, 60, 64, 88, 102, 104
cats 98-99
Cecil Tortoise (**105**) 77, 79, 131
Cervone, Tony 137
Chaplin, Charlie 122
Charlie Dog (**131**) 35, 77, 100, 110
Chester (**152**) 60, 97, 101, 113
cine films 128
Chiniquy, Gerry 34
Cicero 51

Mike and Pat try Porky's patience in *The Wearing Of The Grin*.

Clampett, Bob 15, 18, 19, 22, 26, 35, 56, 57, 79, 86, 111, 122, 124
Clarence Cat (**45**)
When Sylvester decides to go "cold Tweety" in *Birds Anonymous*, he seeks the help of Clarence, a reformed bird-hunter who runs an organization dedicated to helping cats to kick the bird habit.
Claude Cat (**78**) 52, 98, 100, 101, 102
Clyde Bunny (**100**)
Bugs' skeptical nephew appears in *His Hare-Raising Tale*, *Yankee Doodle Bugs*, and *Fright Before Christmas*. Ever-skeptical of Bugs' tales of bravado, Clyde doubts his uncle's all he's cracked up to be.
Colonel Rimfire (**127**) 88
Colvig, Pinto 98

comics 35, 50, 51, 64, 71, 78, 83, 85, 86, 103, 104, 125, 130, 131
Commander Flying Saucer X-2 *see* Marvin the Martian 45, 136
computer effects 15
Conrad Cat (**25**) 98
Cookie 107
Cool Cat (**126**) 77, 88
Cottontail Smith (**193**)
In *Super Rabbit*, a heroic, flying Bugs Bunny must stop this Texas rabbit hater from mass extermination. Unfortunately, in the battle that follows, Bugs manages to lose some super carrots to the enemy.
Count Bloodcount (**6**) 85, 96
Crackpot Quail (**168**)
Willoughby the hunting dog is outclassed by *The Crackpot Quail*. But while the nutty, practical-joking bird will not be caught, he, at least, leads Willoughby to another prize doggie catch—a whole lot of trees.
Crusher (**130**) 97
Curt Martin (**139**) 19, 21

D

Daffy Duck (**40**) 9, 11, 16, 21, 22-23, 24-25, 26-27, 28-29, 33, 34, 37, 38, 48, 52, 61, 62,71, 85, 88, 90, 93, 96, 97, 110, 111, 113, 116, 117, 123, 125, 132, 133, 134-135
as Duck Dodgers 26, 35, 44, 45, 136, 137
Daisy Lou (**67**) 16, 51
Dalton, Timothy 132
Dan Backslide 97
Dante, Joe 133
Daphne Duck *see* Mrs. Daffy Duck
De Guard, Philip 114, 115, 121
Dini, Paul 137
Disney, Walt 37, 86, 106, 107, 110
Dr. I.Q. Hi 136, 137
Dr. Jekyll 21, 59, 97, 101
Dr. Seuss (Theodore Geisel) 124

The numbered character chart (above) is the key to the endpapers at the start and finish of the book. See how many characters you know, and spot your favorites!

Dodo Bird (**79**) 84
Dodsworth the Cat (**82**)
In *Kiddin' The Kitten* and *A Peck O'Trouble*, big fat Dodsworth wants to avoid the work of catching mice and birds—so he "teaches" the Kitten to do it for him. When plans go awry, little cat goes AWOL and big cat suffers.
dogs 100-101
Donald Duck 107
Dora Standpipe 97
Dougherty, Joe 32
Doyle, Larry 137
Duck Dodgers TV series 35, 45, 136, 137
Duck Soup 122
Dumbo 120

E

Eager Beaver (**87**)
Ski-capped and buck-toothed, *The Eager Beaver* is super-devoted to his colony's beaver dam. After first felling telephone poles to add to the dam's logs, Eager finally brings down a giant redwood in the nick of time.
Easter Rabbit 20, 105

Grover Groundhog in *One Meat Brawl*

A member of the Gas-House Gorillas gets ready to play dirty in *Baseball Bugs*.

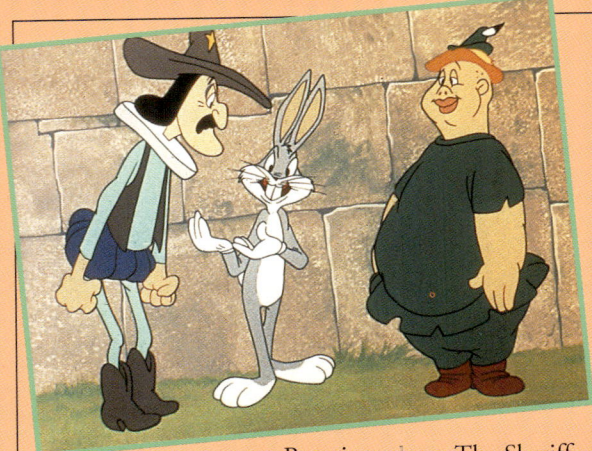

Bugs introduces The Sheriff of Nottingham to Little John in *Rabbit Hood*.

Easy Peckin's Fox **(102)**
In *Easy Peckin's*, this rogue reynard's chicken thievery is halted by big, tough George Rooster. Fox finally attempts to seduce a hen into the pot, promising her various finery. Miss Chicken does end up with a fancy fox stole—but it's our hero's fur.

Edward G. Robbersome 123
Egghead **(140)** 23, 53, 116
Egghead Jr. **(99)** 47, 51
Elfman, Jenna 132
Elmer Fudd **(41)** 9, 14, 16, 17, 18, 19, 20, 23, 25, 28, 29, 30, 36, 37, 48, 50, 60, 61, 90, 91, 101, 104, 105, 118, 122, 125, 129, 130,
Emily *see* Agatha and Emily
Emmerich, Robert D. 32

F

Fabrette *see* Penelope
Fantasia 37, 86, 118
Fields, W.C. 122, 123
Fifi **(169)** 43
Fifth-Column Mouse 103
Flash Gordon 45
Flat Foot Flooky 35
Fluffy 106
Flying Kitten, the **(22)**
Go Fly A Kit tells how this catkin was raised by an "eagle with an overdeveloped mother instinct." Kitten sees a cute girl cat pursued by a bulldog, then uses his powers of flight to beat the bully back.

Foghorn Leghorn **(97)** 9, 29, 46, 47, 51, 60, 61, 85, 86, 111, 112
Foray, June 20, 43, 62, 113
Foster, Warren 58, 63, 85, 111, 113
Fox **(106)**
A Fox In A Fix enrolls for watchdog lessons with chicken guard Hector the bulldog. Fox's plan is to steal, not protect the birds—but after several efforts backfire, it's the Fox who needs protection.

A strange horn-head wanders through *Porky In Wackyland*.

Foxy 106
Francois **(60)** 21
Franklyn, Milt 118, 121
Fraser, Brendan 123, 132
Freberg, Stan 61, 80, 83, 86, 102, 105, 113
Fred Sheepdog 72
Freleng, Isadore "Friz" 32, 34, 40, 58, 60, 61, 62, 75, 79, 89, 110, 111, 122, 124
Frisky Puppy **(145)** 98, 101

G

Gabby Goat 33
Gable, Clark 122
Gambling Bug **(185)** 99, 105
Gas-House Gorillas, the **(118)**
This team of baseball-playing brutes destroys the opposition Tea Totalers in *Baseball Bugs*. Totalers fan Bugs Bunny claims the Gorillas play dirty—and is challenged to take the thuggish team on himself.

General Krutchat-kuh S'am *see* Yosemite Sam
Genie **(11)** 29
George, the cat 99
George, the fox **(144)** 101
Gerry **(58)**
When Bugs pursues the Singing Sword in *Knighty Knight Bugs*, Black Knight Sam pursues Bugs astride Gerry, his faithful dragon. Or not so faithful: Gerry's a cold-ridden beast whose sneezes prove painful for his knight rider.

Gertrude Calculus *see* Professor Calvin Q. Calculus and Gertrude Calculus
Giant **(57)**
In *Jack-Wabbit And The Beanstalk*, this goofy goliath battles Bugs for possession of his own giant carrots—and comes out an economy size loser. The Giant is so big, 20 steps take him all the way around the world.

Giovanni Jones **(122)** 95
Girl Mouse *see* Boy and Girl Mouse
Goldberg, Eric 133
"Golden Carrot" award 112
Goldimouse **(94)**
In *Goldimouse And The Three Cats*, this blonde rodent invades the home of Sylvester, Mrs. Sylvester, and "spoiled brat" Sylvester Jr., who catch the mouse. After Goldi's escape, Jr. goes back to eating porridge.

Goofy Gophers: Mac **(176)** and Tosh **(177)** 22, 29, 77, 80, 81, 113
Goopy Geer 107
Gossamer **(117)** 87
Granny **(92)** 48, 50, 58, 59, 62, 113, 132
Green Lantern 137
Greenstreet, Sydney 123
Gretel **(134)** 20
Gribbrock, Robert 114
Grover Groundhog **(192)**
Grover Groundhog spends Groundhog Day evading hunter Porky Pig and his dog in *One Meat Brawl*. When, finally, they have him cornered, Grover fights them off using his shadow-boxing skills.

Gruesome Gorilla **(123)** 21, 84

H

Halberg, Gladys 34
Ham and Ex 32
Hansel **(133)** 20
Hardaway, Ben 14
Hardy, Oliver 123
Harmon, Hugh 106, 107, 110

Harris, Ken 121, 133
Hassan **(115)** 29
Hatfield **(109)** and McCoy **(111)**, a.k.a. The Feudin' Mountain Boys
In *Feud With A Dude*, Merlin the Magic Mouse flies his magic carpet into Ozark Mountains and is attacked by these zany hillbillies—who get themselves transformed into chickens and other barnyard beasts.

Hatta Mari 96
Hausen, Bernie 78
Hector 105
Henery Hawk **(98)** 9, 46, 47, 61, 64, 77, 84, 85, 130

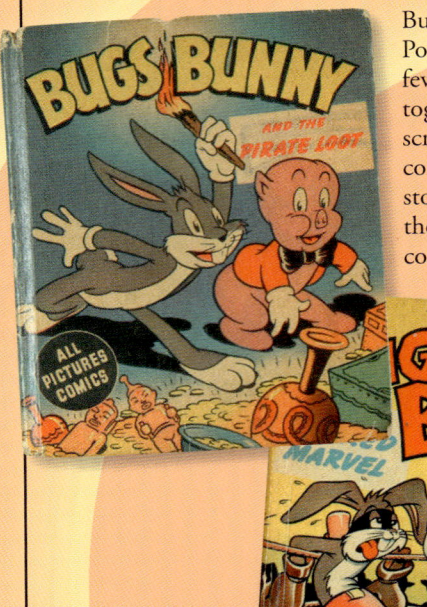

Bugs Bunny and Porky Pig made few appearances together on screen—but in comics and storybooks, they've been great companions.

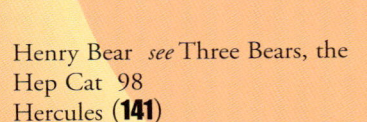

Henry Bear *see* Three Bears, the
Hep Cat 98
Hercules **(141)**
This thuggish construction worker uproots Bugs' rabbit hole, leaving him a *Homeless Hare*—and priming the rabbit for delicious revenge. Cement vats and falling steel casings ultimately seal Hercules' fate.

Hiawatha **(76)**
By the shores of Gitche-Gumee lives this little hunter in *Hiawatha's Rabbit Hunt*. Efforts to catch Bugs result in Hiawatha's downfall—but the brave kisses Bugs to show he hasn't been totally beaten.

High Note **(174)** 112
Hippety Hopper **(39)** 57, 60, 61, 62, 63
"Hollywood" Wolf 122
Honey Bee *see* Moth
Honey (Bosko's girlfriend) 106
Honey Bunny 51
Honey (Yosemite Sam's wife) **(27)** 41
Honey-Mousers, the: Ralph **(178)**, Morton **(179)**, and Alice **(180)** 103, 113
Hoodlum Pigs, the **(158, 159, 160)**
In *The Windblown Hare* and *The Turn-Tale Wolf*, these three little fairy-tale rejects beat up a weakling wolf and sell their cheap houses of straw and sticks to Bugs Bunny. That last move is, of course, a mistake...

Hubie **(171)** 52, 98, 102, 113

140

I

Infant Tom Thumb (51)
In *I Was A Teenage Thumb*, tiny Tom is born to George Thumb and wife Prunehilda. Out for a medieval pram ride, the mini-baby is attacked by cat, bird, and fish—but escapes to be knighted by the King.

"Inki" cartoons 84
Instant Martians (10) 45, 136
Ising, Rudolph 106, 107, 110

J

Joe Glow (2)
The title character of *Joe Glow, The Firefly* is a curious bug in a fireman's cap. Sneaking round a darkened campground, Joe tries not to wake the giant humans. Until he departs, that is—yelling a final "Good night!" at a snoring camper.

Jones, Chuck 14, 19, 20, 21, 22, 26, 27, 28, 35, 42, 44, 47, 50, 60, 64, 65, 70, 72, 73, 74, 78, 82, 84, 85, 87, 89, 90, 91, 94, 95, 102, 104, 105, 107, 110, 111, 117, 118, 119, 120, 123, 124, 125, 133
Jose Crow (4) 48, 49
Junior (156) and Little Girl (157)
After mistreating a dog in *A Waggily Tale*, human boy Junior dreams of having been transformed into a pet-store pooch. Junior figures a dog's life will be easy, but his little girl buyer shows him otherwise in a series of childish hijinks.

Junyer Bear *see* Three Bears, the

K

K-9, Lieutenant (12) 44, 75, 136
Keaton, Buster 122
Kid Banty (137) 46, 47
Killer Diller 97
Kitten, the (80)
This cute little kitty takes lessons in mouse catching from Dodsworth the Cat in *Kiddin' The Kitten* and *A Peck O' Trouble*.

L

Laughing Hippo (155)
In *Hamateur Night* and *Bacall To Arms*, this lug of a theater audience member heckles patron and performer alike with his gargantuan girth and gut-busting guffaws.

Daydreaming again: Ralph Phillips in *From A to Z-Z-Z-Z*.

Laurie Becool 122
"Legs" Rhinestone 97
Levitow, Abe 89
Little Blabbermouse (104)
On a mice's tour of a department store, *Little Blabbermouse* drives the tour guide to distraction with his constant chatter, until a cat puts in an appearance and brings the tour to an abrupt end.

Steamboat Piggy takes the riverboat wheel in *Hittin' The Trail To Hallelujah Land*.

Little Ghost *see* Big Ghost and Little Ghost
Little Girl *see* Junior and Little Girl
Little Kitty 32
lobby cards 116, 117
Locklear, Heather 132
Lola Bunny (196) 50, 51
Looney Tunes
  birth of 106
  compilations 117
  guiding principles 110
  in foreign languages 48, 116
  in wartime 124, 125
  Looney Tunes: Back In Action 123, 132-136
  title music for 22
  trademark 33
Lorre, Peter 123
Lo, the Poor Indian (136)
Merlin the Magic Mouse meets this tough but dopey warrior in *Hocus Pocus Pow Wow*. Lo wants Merlin for the magic turkey dinners his hat can produce—but the Indian ends up with no gobblers to gobble.

Louie (61) 21
Love, Harry 119
Lovy, Alex 89
Lucas, George 45

M

Ma Bear *see* Three Bears, the
Mac *see* Goofy Gophers, the
Malcom Falcon (107)
In *Road To Andalay*, Sylvester hunts Speedy with this burly bird of prey and lives to regret it. In the end, salt on the bird's tail causes it to fall off... along with Sylvester's and Speedy's tails.

Mam'selle Kitty *see* Penelope the cat
Maltese, Michael 118
Manuel Crow (3) 48, 49
Maquettes 15, 59
Marc Antony (96) 50, 98, 99, 100, 103
Mars Exploration Rover Mission 137
Martian (14) 89
Martin, Larry 111
Martin, Steve 123, 132
Marvin the Martian (9) 9, 44, 45, 75, 110, 132, 136, 137
Marx, Groucho 122
Mary Jane 78, 131
McCoy *see* Hatfield and McCoy
McKimson, Robert 14, 15, 19, 21, 23, 25, 26, 39, 46, 47, 49, 51, 56, 61, 63, 85, 86, 89, 91, 111, 112, 124, 131
McKimson, Charles 131
McKimson, Tom 131
Mechanical Rabbit (63)
In *Hare-Raising Hare*, this long-eared girl droid is bait to lure Bugs Bunny to a mad scientist's lair. In the end, the rab-bot's mechanical nature revealed, Bugs romances her anyway. "So it's mechanical!"

merchandise 84, 128, 129
Merlin The Magic Mouse (167) 89
Merrie Melodies cartoons 106
mice 102-103
Michigan J. Frog (50) 94, 110
Mickey Mouse 106, 128
Mighty Angelo (35) 105
Mike (162) and Pat (161)
In *The Wearing Of The Grin*, weary traveler Porky stays at an Irish inn and dreams he's in the clutches of these two tricky leprechauns and their h-h-hideous magic green shoes. Or WAS it a dream?

Millicent (132)
Elmer's Uncle Judd pays him $500 to babysit this giant Slobovian rabbit in *Rabbit Romeo*. The Romeo of the title is Bugs—drafted in to woo Millicent when the oversized femme seeks a husband.

Minah Bird (89) 84
Mischa the Slobovian Mouse (181)
In *Mouse Mazurka*, this little rodent causes chaos for Sylvester in a old-time Russian province. Finally dodging the cat by blowing himself into the hereafter, now-ghostly Mischa is spooked when Sylvester promptly does the same.

Miss Prissy (73) 47, 51, 113
Mr. and Mrs. Wilbur 105
Mr. Lovebird (34)
In *Life With Feathers*, this romantic fowl is left loveless after a fight with his wife. Mr. Lovebird decides to end it all in a cat's jaws—but Sylvester is too suspicious to go along with the plan.

Morrow, Jackie 107
Morton *see* Honey-Mousers, the
Moth (183), Honey Bee (184), and Black Widow Spider (182)
In *Eatin' On The Cuff*, insect chivalry is called for when the man-hungry Widow Spider catches Moth on his wedding day. Now bride-to-bee Honey must fight off the devious dowager.

Mot the Martian baby (8) 105
Mouse (72) 99
Mrs. Bugs Bunny 51
Mrs. Daffy Duck 51, 85

The singing giraffe records her songs in *Nelly's Folly*.

Mrs. Elmer Fudd (**153**) 50
Mrs. Gorilla 21
Mrs. Sylvester J. Pussycat (**84**) 60
Murray, Bill 123
Murray, Carmen "Max" 106
Murray, Johnny 106

N
NASA 39, 137
Nasty Canasta (**189**) 20, 27
National Film Register 118
Nelly (**62**) 89
Nelson, Dick 123
Nero Lion (**70**) 21
Night watch-cat 98
Noble, Maurice 89, 118
Nordli, Ernie 115

O
Oliver Owl (**15**) 32, 98
O'Loughlin, Tom 115
Orville (**38**)
  In *Lost And Foundling*, Sniffles raises an orphan egg into a childish giant hawk. Orville briefly turns bad guy upon learning that hawks eat mice, but in the end can't bear to bite the mousey hand that fed him.
Oscars 42, 47, 48, 49, 58, 110, 111, 117
Owl Jolson 84

P
Papa Owl 78
Pasquale (**116**)
  This long-suffering Pisa pizza and pasta chef is dogged by Charlie Dog in A Hound For Trouble. But Pasquale refuses to adopt the pooch as his pet. "Whatsamatter with you?" Charlie sings.
Pat *see* Mike and Pat
Paul Puma (Pete Puma's cousin) 86
Penelope the cat (**91**) 43, 50
Pepe Le Moko 43
Pepe Le Pew (**90**) 9, 42, 43, 110, 111
Pete and Re-Pete 125
Pete Puma (**146**) 86, 93, 113
Petunia Pig (**44**) 35, 51

Daffy wants Nasty Canasta's attention in *My Little Duckaroo*.

Philbert 89
Pierce, Tedd 111
Piggy 106
Pistol-nose Pringle 97
Pizza-puss Lasagne 97
Pizzicato Pussy Cat (**71**) 99
Playboy Penguin (**103**) 94, 95
Pluto 106
Popeye 107
Porky Pig (**43**) 9, 22, 23, 27, 32-35, 57, 60, 62, 98, 99, 100, 103, 110, 114, 123, 125, 128
  as Space Cadet 35, 136
  posters 117
Pratt, Hawley 114
Prince Chow Mein 53
printed advertisements 117
Professor Calvin Q. Calculus (**86**) and Gertrude Calculus (**85**)
  In *The Hole Idea*, Professor Calculus is the proud inventor of the portable hole. Nagging wife Gertrude doesn't appreciate the breakthrough—until a fall through one sends her to Hades.
Professor Fritz Owl 84
Puddy-dog *see* Spike
publishing 130-131
Pumpkinhead Martin (**138**) 19, 21
Puppy *see* Butch J. Bulldog and Puppy
Pussyfoot (**93**) 50, 98, 99, 100, 103

Q
Quentin Quail (**190**) and Toots (**191**)
  In *Quentin Quail*, papa bird Quentin struggles to catch a worm for his baby Toots. Unlike many a Termite-Terrace predator, Quentin succeeds in his hunt—but Toots refuses to eat a worm that "looks like Frank Sinatra"!

R
Rags McMutt 100
Ralph *see* Honey-Mousers, the
Ralph Phillips (**37**) 105, 125
Ralph Wolf 72, 73, 74
Rapid Rabbit 89
Rattled Rooster (**194**)
  The Rattled Rooster gets that way by chasing a turtlenecked worm through a series of unsuccessful trapping efforts. Predator and prey briefly unite to stop a hungry rattlesnake—but moments later it's back to war.
Ravishing Ronald 97
record albums 112, 113, 129
Red (**59**)
  Warners' wackiest fairy-tale character is this brassy, bespectacled bobbysoxer in *Little Red Riding Rabbit*. Butchering her lines—"That's an awfully big nose for you ta have!"—Red is so annoying that Bugs would rather punish her than the Wolf.
Red Hot Ryder (**114**) and his horse (**113**)
  In *Buckaroo Bugs*, "Brooklyn's famous fighting cowboy" is this dopey range rider with an even dopier horse. Red's efforts to capture Masked Marauder Bugs are doomed to failure from the word giddap.
Red Riding Hood (**186**)
  Granny's granddaughter in *Red Riding Hoodwinked* is a modern-day, bus-riding version of the fairy-tale tot. With Tweety in tow, Red is endangered both by the big, bad wolf and the big, bad puddy tat.
Red Riding Wolf (**77**)
  In *Pigs In A Polka* and *Little Riding Rabbit*, this lunch-happy lobo first chases three pigs to a

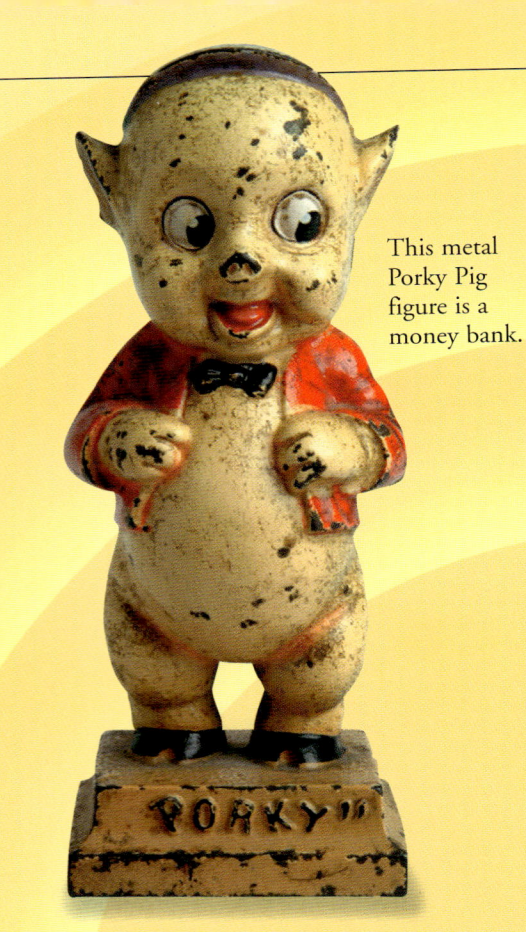

This metal Porky Pig figure is a money bank.

Hungarian rhapsody score—then buries the hatchet with Bugs to get even with the ever-annoying Red.
Reed, Shirley 35
Roach, Hal 32
Road Runner (**53**) 9, 48, 52, 53, 64, 66-67, 68, 70, 71, 72, 74, 110, 130, 137
Roberts, Bill 94
Robinson, Edward G. 123
Rocky (Edward G. Robinson caricature) 123
Rocky (**32**) and Mugsy (**33**) 96
Rogers, Kent 122, 123
Roxy 123
Russian dog 101

S
Sam (Sylvester's pal) 61
Sam Sheepdog (**83**) 72, 73, 74
Schlesinger, Leon 128, 130
Scott, Raymond 113
Scribner, Rod 56, 111
Seaman Hook 124
Second Banana (**166**) 89
Senor Vulturo (**19**) 48
Selzer, Eddie 21
She-Devil (**42**) 39, 50
Sheriff of Nottingham (**188**)
  In *Rabbit Hood*, carrot poacher Bugs tricks the scheming Sheriff into building a summer home in the King's garden. Also heckling the Sheriff is oafish Little John, forever warning that Robin Hood will soon arrive.
Sheriff, the (**135**)
  When Bunny and Claude go carrot-robbing in the Wild West, it's this pugnacious redneck who tracks them down. Too bad for justice—the long arms of this lawman are too short to reach the antihero hares.
Silly Symphonies 106
Sinestro 137
Skelton, Red 40

Slick Fox (**30**)
  This con man invades Foghorn's farm in *Fox Terror*, hoping to raid the hen coop behind Barnyard Dawg's back. Slick uses Foghorn to distract Dawg from the poultry—but the rooster catches on and gets revenge in the end.
Slowpoke Rodriguez 49
Slug McSlug 97
Smokey the Genie (**13**)
  A-Lad-In His Lamp finds Bugs rubbing a lamp to bring forth the genie. Smokey tends to be summoned from his lamp at the wrong moment: the genie is caught first bathing, then smooching a girl.
Snafu, Private 124
Sniffles the Mouse (**101**) 78, 99, 104, 110
Snooks 99
Snow White 120
Sour Puss 99
Speedy Gonzales (**47**) 48-49, 60, 61, 85, 99, 103, 110, 111
Spike (**151**) 58, 59, 60, 62, 101, 113
Squirrel (**48**)
  This forest rodent tries very hard to open a coconut in *Much Ado About Nutting*—finally dropping it from a skyscraper when all else fails.
Stalling, Carl 113, 124

Left to right: Groovy, Ham, and Bacon, a.k.a. The Three Little Bops

Star Johnson 137
Star Wars 45
Steve Brody (**154**)
  Steve thinks a rabbit's foot mascot might be just the thing to end his run of bad luck in *Bowery Bugs*. But, he picks the wrong rabbit—Bugs—and soon finds his luck going from bad to worse.
Stinky 42
Storch, Larry 88, 89
story meeting 119
Sutherland, Sid 111
Suzanne (**29**)
  In *A Kiddie's Kitty*, this playful little girl rescues weary Sylvester from a dog's pursuit. But Suzanne's childish misbehavior winds up frazzling the cat further. Suzanne also starred in a long-running series of Looney Tunes comic-book stories.
Sylvester (**56**) 9, 35, 48, 57, 58-61, 74, 75, 97, 99, 103, 110
  his baby mouse son (**54**) 60
  his cat friends (**64, 65, 66**) 57
  his voice 57
Sylvester Jr. (**95**) 62, 63

T

Tashlin, Frank 111, 124
Tasmanian Devil (**88**) 9, 18, 38, 39, 111
Taylor, Deems 37
Taz *see* Tasmanian Devil
Technical Fairy First Class 124
"Teeth" Malloy 97
Termite Terrace 107
theater bills 116-117
Thomas *see* Sylvester
Thomas Cat 98
Thomas, Richard H. 114, 115
Thorson, Charles 78
Three Bears, the: Junyer (**75**) Ma (**74**), and Henry (**81**) 82, 83
Three Little Bops, the: Groovy (**163**), Ham (**164**), and Bacon (**165**)
  Little Pig are a cool jazz band who won't let the Big Bad Wolf join—until he visits Hades and becomes a much hepper shadow of his former self.
Thurber, James 86
Tom Corbett 45
Tommy Cat *see* Night watch-cat
Tommy Turtle 32
Tom Thumb (**31**)
  Tom Thumb In Trouble sees a three-inch-high boy nearly drowned in a tub of dishwater. He is saved by a bird—but his woodcutter dad mistakenly blames birdie for having caused the trouble to begin with.
Toots *see* Quentin Quail and Toots
Tosh *see* Goofy Gophers
Towser 107
Tough Little Bird (**28**)
  When two dogs sneak around a theater in *Stage Fright*, they meet this scrappy inhabitant of a magician's hat. The bird shows his irritation at being disturbed by bopping the dogs with their bone.
Tuff (**150**)
  Traveling through Rattlesnake Gulch in *The Fistic Mystic*, Merlin the Magic Mouse is challenged by this bandit. Bad move by the bandit—once a pair of magic boxing gloves ends up on the attack.
Tweety (**55**) 9, 57, 56, 58-59, 60, 62, 74, 75, 110, 111, 113, 123, 132
Tytla, Bill 118

U

Uncle Ham 51

V

Van Citters, Darrel 86
vaudeville 91

Cutley and china run from the dough monster in *The Dish Ran Away With The Spoon*.

This model chart is from *Tortilla Flaps*.

video cassettes and games 39
Vulture 84

W

Wagner, Richard 119, 121
Warner Bros. cartoon style 106
Warner Bros. Movie World theme park 45
Wait, Elmer 111
Weasel, the (**175**) 47
Weasel ("Dr.") (**147**) 105
Webb, Danny 123
Wentworth 41
What's Opera, Doc? 110, 118-119, 120-121
Wilber 106
Wile E. Coyote (**52**) 9, 52, 53, 65-71, 72, 74, 75, 110, 130, 132, 137,
Willoughby (**24**) 101
Witch Hazel (**16**) 20, 21, 48, 110, 113
Wood, Cornett 114
Wover (the Fudds' dog) 50
Wyner, Irv 115

Y

"Yes Session" 119
Yosemite Sam (**46**) 8, 13, 18, 40-41, 62, 75, 113, 129, 133, 137
Yob 105

ACKNOWLEDGMENTS

Additional hires artworks:
Desert Hunt (pp. 66-67): Fred Gardner and Dennis Benazales; Bugs' Burrow (pp. 16-17): Fred Gardner, Peter Tumminello, and Dennis Benazales; Ralph and Sam (p. 73), Sniffles (p. 78), Cecil Tortoise (p. 79), Goofy Gophers (p. 80), The Three Bears (p. 82), Pete Puma (p. 86), Cool Cat and Colonel Rimfire (p. 88), A. Flea (p. 104), Pvt. Snafu and Seaman Hook (p. 124): Tony Cervone and Spike Brandt.

Jacket artwork:
David Alvarez; Mike DeCarlo; Keith Aiken

Special photography by:
Joseph Viles

The author would like to thank the following people:

Earl Kress, David Gerstein, Fred Patten, Keith Scott, and Daniel Goldmark, for their expertise and assistance; adding to the insanity were Leonard Maltin, Leith Adams, Martha Sigall, Karl Cohen, Michael Barrier, Steve Schneider, Mike Glad, Mark Kausler, Joe Dante, Eric Goldberg, Will Friedwald, Marea Boylan, Jon Cooke, and Martin Olsen, all of whom deserve special thanks, a laurel, and a hardy handclasp; the Number 1 Team Player would also like to thank his colleagues at Warner Bros. Worldwide Publishing, including Paula Allen, Connie Baldwin, Kevin Bricklin, and Charles Carney. Finally, special thanks to the readers of cartoonresearch.com.

Dorling Kindersley would like to thank the following for their help in producing this book:

Allison Abbate
Amanda Adams
Leith Adams
Paula Allen
Michael Arnold
Constance Baldwin
Edwin Beecroft
Lori Bond
Spike Brandt

Kevin Bricklin
Erica Callahan
Charles Carney
Martha Carreon
Tony Cervone
Joe Dante
Brian Deputy
Christopher DeFaria
Gino Dubois

Marlene Fenton
Steven Fogelson
Jess Garcia
Bernie Goldman
Eric Goldberg
Christopher Grakal
Mark Greenhalgh
Skye Herzog
Claire Jones

Frank Keating
John Kelly
Pat Kowalski
Capt. David Krambeck
Christine Lacy
Laura Marquez
Tad Marburg
Dale Nelson
Melanie O'Brien

Bobby Page
Maria Perez
Rezwan Razani
Isabelle Richard
Dan Romanelli
Julia Schmidt Price
Victoria Selover
Anne Sharples
Denny Singleton

Aditya Sood
Kim Steelsmith
Linda Steiner
Toni Sturdivant
Lila Takayanaga
Cathy Tincknell
Catherine Trillo
Amy Wagner
Mark Whiting

The publisher would like to thank the following for their kind permission to reproduce their photographs:
(Key: a=above; c=center; b=below; l=left; r=right; t=top)

112 Kobal Collection: br; 113 Getty Images: Timelife/ Bill Bridges tc; Hulton Archive/Getty Images: br; Popperfoto: Reuters/Rose Prouser cla; 116 Hulton Archive/Getty Images: Museum of the City of New York/Berenice Abbott/Archive Photos ca; 116-117 Hulton Archive/Getty Images: b; 117 Corbis: Bettmann crb; 119 Mary Evans Picture Library: P. Kalpokas tr; 120 M. Maurice J. and Marjorie H. Noble Living Trust: Courtesy of the Maurice J. and Marjorie H. Noble Trust cra. All other images courtesy of Warner Bros.